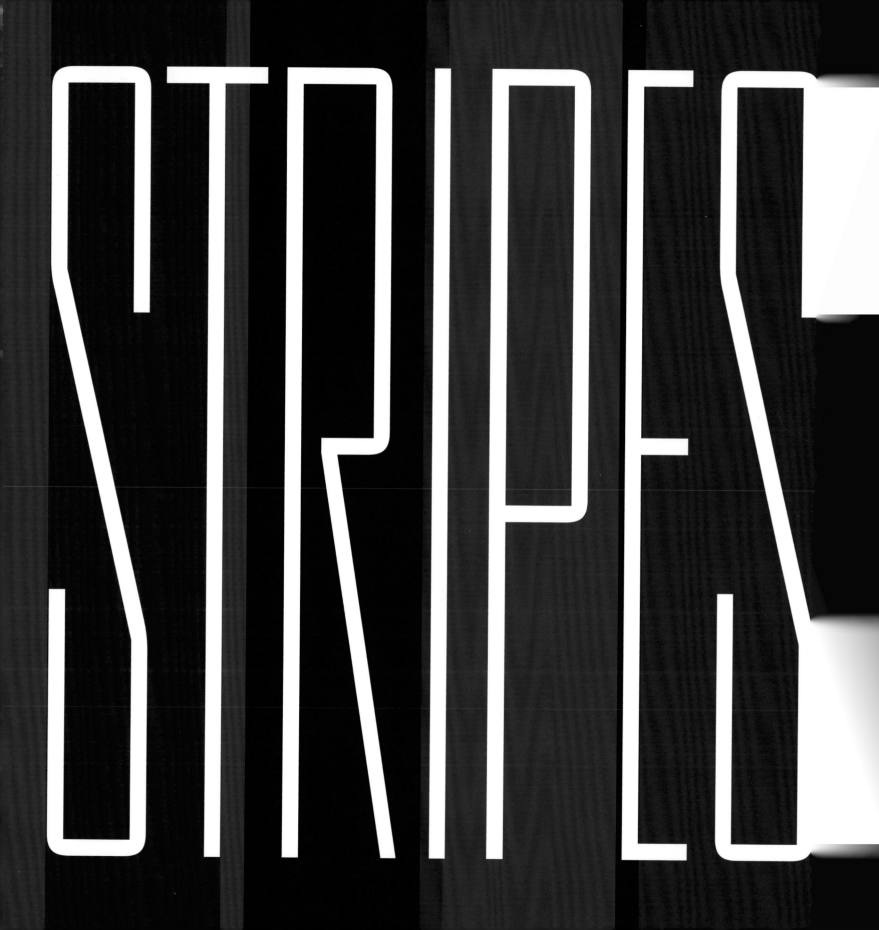

STRIPES:
DESIGN
BETWEEN
THE LINES

LINDA
O'KEEFFE

Thames & Hudson

to Nora

First published in the United Kingdom in 2012 by
Thames & Hudson Ltd, 181A High Holborn,
London WC1V 7QX

Designed by Claudia Brandenburg, Language Arts

British Library Cataloguing-in-Publication Data
A catalogue record for this book is available from the British Library

ISBN: 978-0-500-51669-0

Printed and bound in China

To find out about all our publications, please visit **www.thamesandhudson.com**.
There you can subscribe to our e-newsletter, browse or download our current
catalogue, and buy any titles that are in print.

It's relatively easy to assess the personality of a single line or stripe. According to essayist Alain de Botton, "A straight example . . . signal[s] . . . stable and dull, a wavy one will appear foppish and calm, a jagged one angry and confused." When grouped together, however, stripes are generally perceived as flamboyant, happy souls. Respectfully ancient yet always somehow excitingly modern, their rhythmic repetition is a universally pleasing representation of order and discipline.

The earliest form of decorative striping shows up in Paleolithic caves, alongside mineral-pigment drawings of bison and antelope, as clusters of serpentine-shaped lines or flutings thought to be the tracings left by fingertips dragged across wet clay. The next evolution of prehistoric stripes, found engraved into West African rocks, is heavily symbolic and is considered to be the pictographic precursor of an alphabet.

The earliest purely celebratory vehicles for striped patterns include fabrics, likely due to how easily they can be woven. One remnant uncovered from the Neolithic period carries a border of monochromatic stripes; natural linen excavated from an Egyptian tomb has dainty blue and pink stripes worked into its selvage. Striped clothing is eye-catching by nature, so it invariably singles out

its wearer. A passage in Matthew describes the privileged children of great men who "oft had their garments striped with divers colors."

Printed stripes, on the other hand, didn't truly become popular until the mid-nineteenth century, when hand-blocking and hand-painting gave way to machinery that could mass-produce yardage with stunningly accurate straight lines. Around the same time, the excise duty on printed papers in England was revoked, so the luxury of stenciled wallpapers became available to the masses, and striped rooms cropped up in every class of home throughout Europe and beyond.

In the Middle Ages sumptuary laws restricted furs and gold threads to the garments of the nobility but assigned striped hoods and cloaks to prostitutes to serve as beacons of their immorality. When a small group of mendicant Carmelite monks arrived in Europe, their vertically striped mantles played havoc with societal norms. The stripes reverentially represented the tracks of

the fiery chariot ride the prophet Elijah—their spiritual leader—took to heaven, but nevertheless the brothers were reviled and scorned for their perceived sedition. Heraldry expert Michel

Pastoureau cites the Carmelite scandal as a turning point in the history of stripes and documents a significant period thereafter when only rogues and outcasts wore or were portrayed in striped clothing.

Medievals viewed the body's outer coverings as a reflection of inner spiritual character, and anyone who transgressed in sartorial terms was deemed guilty of committing the sin of vanity. Late medieval artwork also had a tradition of depicting pious people stiffly, against flat backgrounds, and so, according to Pastoureau, when perspective was discovered and represented by strong lines in early Renaissance painting, stripes earned the moniker "the devil's language" because of their inherent vitality and pronounced ability to bring a depth of field to a formerly static canvas. They literally upended the conventional, catholic, two-dimensional way of seeing,

mirroring the larger schisms going on in European society.

In sharp contrast, contemporary clothing, product, and interior designers revere stripes as perennially fashionable, gender neutral, nondenominational, nonageist, and apolitical. Today, they work as well on a clown as on a cardinal; they're as dignified on an ensign as on an admiral. A row of black and white stripes accentuates the elegant cut of a couture gown but epitomizes humiliation when it's multiplied on an outfit that's worn head to toe. The same row of pale blue stripes can either signify "cute" on a baby's bib or "aristocratic" on a silk robe, making them one of the most commercially viable patterns of all time. In film noir lingo, it's the thickness of a suit's stripe that differentiates a good guy from a gangster, a crook from a C.E.O.

Stripes no longer rank as devilish, but they will always be visually duplicitous. Henri Matisse arguably paved the way for later abstract artists when, in 1905, he created

The Green Line, a portrait of his wife's face bisected with a crude green slash instead of a traditional shadow. One incensed critic slammed the artist for defying convention by treating colors as if they were "sticks of dynamite." Op artists notably adopted stripes as leitmotifs in the mid-twentieth century. At that time many critics dismissed their canvases of illusory effects as mere trompe l'œil amusements, but they are now recognized as legitimate explorations of color, space, light, and perception.

Decades later, in 1989, stripes again caused an art world controversy when the National Gallery of Canada bought *Voice of Fire*, an 18-foot-high painting by Barnett Newman for what was perceived as an outrageous price of $1.8 million. The artist intended its three vertical bands—a central cadmium flanked by two ultramarine—as a commentary on the human condition. Critic Harold Rosenberg, articulating the voices of protesters and petitioners, demanded to know, "How could all [our] grandiloquent dramas be seen in the repeated images of a rectangle with stripes?"

"The mother art," architecture, has also always employed strong visual lines. A building is a structural dialogue between horizontal bricks, sashes, and steps and vertical columns and mullions. In effect, architectural stripes define the spaces in which we live every day. The terraced ziggurats of ancient Egypt, Sumeria, and Mexico and Buddhist stupas emphasize a stepped horizontality that reflects our effort and desire to ascend

spiritually. The ancient Greeks satisfied their need for aesthetic order by constructing peristyle colonnades that vertically framed views out to the landscape. Italian Gothic architecture, with its striped vaulting and walls, references earlier Byzantine mosques. Similarly the eighteenth-century Georgian and American Colonial styles revived the classical fascination with symmetry. In the nineteenth century, the impressive spans of suspension bridges began to slice through the landscape; later, streamlined, parallel horizontal stripes characterized the frenetic rhythm of the 1930s. In the twentieth century, industrial advancements in building materials and modernism's focus on pragmatic

structures led to the verticality of steel-and-glass skyscrapers.

Interior designers through the ages have always capitalized on the stripe's ability to visually exaggerate or diminish a room's size or to set mood. Stripes can rise to formal occasions or curtsy to frivolous garden parties. As a motif, their popularity peaked during the late eighteenth and early nineteenth centuries, when the neoclassical style of Louis XVI affected English Regency and American Federal styles and, in a distilled form, provided the foundation for Swedish Gustavian.

The social significance of stripes has ebbed and flowed for humans according to the day's politics and aesthetics, but Mother Nature has consistently exploited the stripe's graphic ability to camouflage, attract, or defend. Whether it is viewed as pleasantly superficial or deeply fraught with meaning, the stripe's capacity for expression is undeniable. "Because the straight line results from the initiative of a single, unopposed

force, its domain is that of the lyric," says writer Michel Henry. "When two forces are present and thus in conflict, as is the case with the curve or zigzag line,

we are in the domain of drama." Stripes have a theatrical ability to glorify, demean, enliven, dichotomize, identify, move, amuse, deceive, heighten, widen, and solidify anything and everything they adorn. We truly live in a parallel universe.

Left to right: The most memorable of the Academy Award–winning costumes Cecil Beaton designed for the 1964 musical film adaptation of *My Fair Lady* are the black-and-white gowns worn by Audrey Hepburn and the ladies in the Royal Ascot scene. Red-and-white-striped caution or safety tape is the universal nonverbal way to say "Keep Out!" The UPC socks Peter Rittenhouse designs for Ozone are colorful takes on barcode symbology. The banded tops Elvis Presley and the cast wore in the 1957 MGM movie *Jailhouse Rock* resembled summery Breton T-shirts more than standard prison garb; classic "bee-striped" uniforms have disappeared, although one institution in Arizona reintroduced them as a badge of shame for inmates. Lisa Whatmough, who claims to have a very British design sensibility, showcases a fondness for every ticking of every stripe in the design of her bespoke Squint sofa. The disruptive coloration of a tiger butterfly's high-contrast markings disorients predators. Candy canes came into existence in the early nineteenth century; their red stripes are thought to represent either the love of Christ or his spilled blood.

A rainbow, a continuous spectrum of color that is perceived as a striped arc, is universally acknowledged as miraculous; it is a thing of awe to anyone who beholds it. The broad spectrum of monochromatic stripes appropriated from that natural phenomenon dots awnings, cabanas, deck chairs, and striped umbrellas on beaches from Brighton to Bondi, and conjures up a similar sense of innocence and a joie de vivre that's shorthand for a carefree, sociable vacation.

Stripes that evoke another sort of entertainment, those on festive circus tents, have no connection whatsoever to temporary regiment encampments or stripes associated with military uniforms. Yet the two genres merged in the early nineteenth century when pampered bedchambers and drawing rooms in fashionable homes across Europe masqueraded as luxurious, tasseled versions of the elaborate campaign housing sometimes erected.

The multicolored, striped, onion-shaped domes of Saint Basil's Cathedral in Moscow's Red Square recall the exuberant folly of those fashion-conscious tents, although they predate them considerably. They resemble swirly turbans but actually are meant to represent the Heavenly Kingdom as depicted in the Book of Revelation of St. John the Divine.

The cathedral's fifteenth-century patron, who is fondly remembered for speaking his mind to the czar, was a pious man rather than a silly or witty fool, but the patterns that pay him homage elevate the moods of the tourists who throng to the site.

Stripes played their part in one of the most controversial fashion shows ever produced. Elsa Schiaparelli built her 1938 collection around a circus theme even as the world was about to go to war. The designer's decision to dress models in jaunty clown hats and tented veils was viewed as insensitive and perverse. During the runway show, balloon-shaped handbags emerged alongside suits appliquéd with diagonally striped fur and shirts embroidered with cavorting acrobats, posing elephants, and prancing dogs. After war broke out in 1939, Schiaparelli emblazoned striped regimental flags onto blouses and evening gowns as a redemptive salute to French patriotism. In retrospect and removed from a political context, her Circus collection was brilliant.

History has not been so kind, however, to the controversial collection of postmodern furniture launched by Ettore Sottsass and the Memphis Group in the early 1980s. Intended to be both kitsch and futuristic at once, the collective's flamboyant, off-kilter objects utilized candy-colored, striped laminates, crass suburban motifs, and fake snakeskin in an ironic antidote to the staid, soulless objects that were then considered in "good taste." It was perceived as surprisingly ugly even when it debuted, and when Christian Dior later revived interest in the group by basing the entire fall/winter 2011 collection on its cone shapes, stripes, and bold pastels, the clothing was similarly panned. Unlike Paul Cézanne, apparently not everyone sees the delight of living in a "rainbow of chaos."

The vibrantly swirled and striped cupolas of St. Basil's Cathedral in Moscow's Red Square, above, contrast sharply with its dimly lit, mazelike interior. A rainbow, left, has come to symbolize different things to different cultures: nirvana, renewed hope, or a multicolored monster that's intent on eating children. A circus tent's wide stripes, left below, are graphic crowd-pleasers.

For *Le Vent Souffle Où Il Veut*, a temporary installation on the beach in De Haan, Belgium, in 2009, French artist Daniel Buren installed a battalion of striped windsocks on one hundred 36-foot-high flagpoles. Spaced 6.5 feet apart, the masts formed a regimented, 60-square-foot "forest." Buren, renowned for working exclusively with stripes, believes they "divest color of all emotional and anecdotal import," but the spectrum he chose here filled viewers with joy. All of Buren's work features 3.5-inch cabana stripes, his first inspiration. He often sequences stripes by placing them in alphabetical order by color name, thereby achieving what one critic described as "the repetitiveness of reggae."

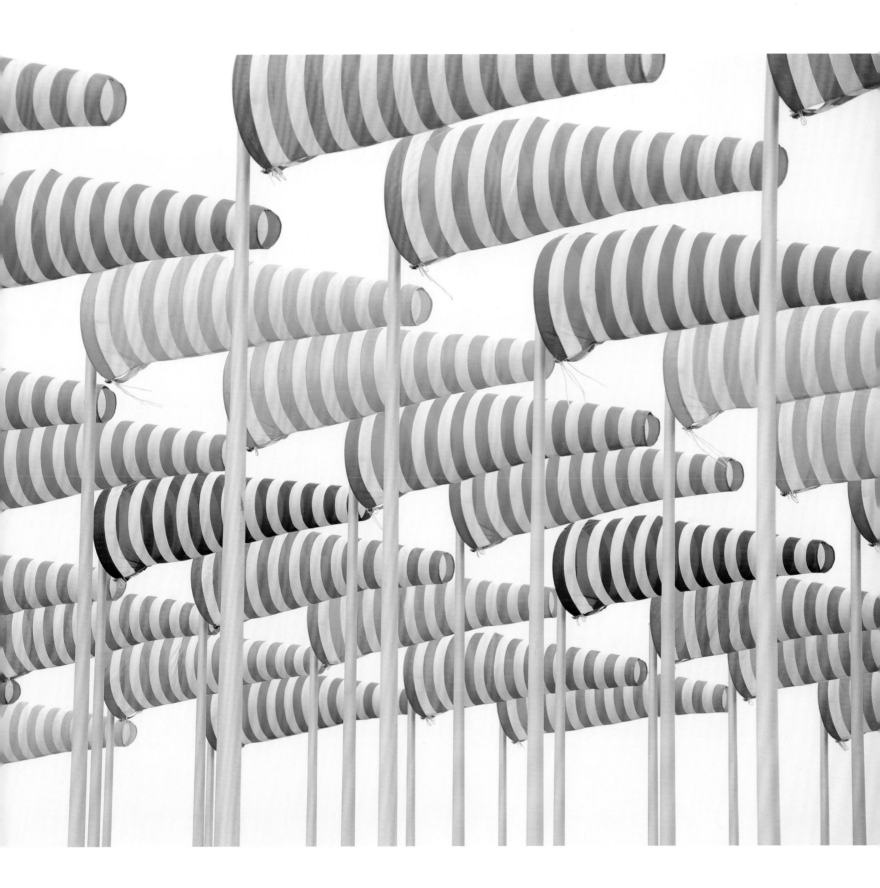

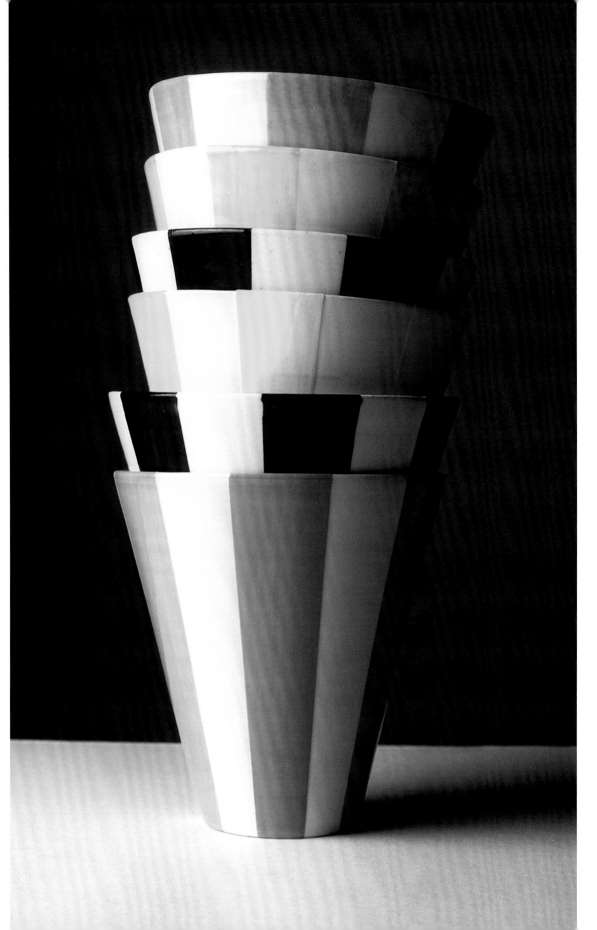

Stripes in every variation of color and thickness are signature embellishments of the vases, pet dishes, canisters, carpets, pillows, and lamp bases Jonathan Adler designs. He wheel-throws his cabana-inspired stoneware tumblers in Peru and finishes them with a glossy white glaze. "I simply wanted them to be bright, colorful, and happy," he says.

As in this community of beach huts in Nazare, Portugal, striped cabanas and lightweight tentlike structures dot beach resorts and private pool decks across the world, providing bathers with momentary privacy or refuge from the sun, wind, and rain. Stripes in seaside settings, interestingly, have no apparent historical or cultural significance.

Over a long career American artist Kenneth Noland consistently produced canvases full of chevrons and stripes, but critics first saw him as a color field painter, then as an abstract expressionist, and finally as a minimalist. Color was his generating force and *Mercury (Ray Parker's Green in the Shadow of Red)* is as vibrant today as it was when he painted it in 1962. By keeping his work abstract, Noland aimed to help viewers bypass allusions and experience his compositions as pure sensation.

Interior designer Christopher Coleman often applies a painterly hand to his rooms and saw ivory mica wallpaper as a natural backdrop for pops of color and stripes in a 3,600-square-foot loft he designed in Manhattan's Flatiron District. In the dining room, he lacquered a striped motif onto a B & B Italia table with auto body paint and paired it with an ottoman that's dressed in a kente-like, randomly striped Donghia fabric. In the living room, abstracted paisley swirls decorate a Ta Ping rug and spar with a circular metal charger that has constructivist roots.

The angle of light often makes the brightly pigmented sheets of corrugated and perforated aluminum at Maison Plastique, Peter Stamberg and Paul Aferiat's weekend house, appear to be striped. The architects list Marcel Breuer, Charles Gwathmey, and Ellsworth Kelly as inspirations for the structure. At 1,100 square feet, this Shelter Island retreat calls to mind Mies van der Rohe's Barcelona Pavilion as well. Here leaning, translucent panels and ceilings that pitch to 14 feet blur the observer's ability to easily distinguish exterior from interior spaces. The property conjures up associations of Cubist paintings or a neon house of cards that's on the verge of toppling.

18

First introduced at Bergdorf Goodman in 1991, Gene Meyer's silk neckwear collection combines the classic shape of an Hermès tie with the vibrancy of Matisse paper cutouts. His naïve, geometric designs appear to be hand-drawn and spontaneous, but in fact the printing process requires scrutiny to ensure that the silk screens don't fall out of register and let traces of white ground silk show through. The store's initial offering sold out within weeks, and to this day the ties are hotly collected and cherished for their elemental celebration of shape and color (left to right: 1996, 1995, 1993, 1992, 1995, 1994, 1992). Certain fans have an agenda to acquire every style in every colorway ever made.

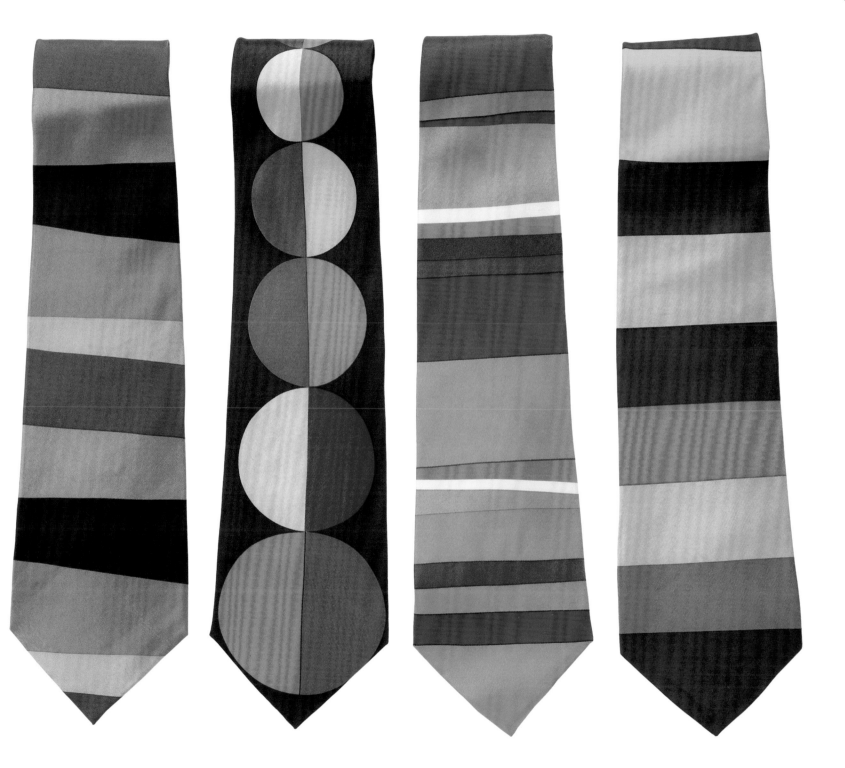

From shoes to cars, Kat O'Sullivan paints everything she owns as a natural extension of her colorful life. Her ramshackle, 1840s Catskills house is no exception; its palette is composed of close to forty colors—not including the shades she mixed on the fly. It came naturally, so to speak, after she walked into a local paint store and ordered one of everything. Needless to say, she received a standing ovation from the owners on her way out. The wood siding dictated the facade's rectilinear design and makes the perceptibly tilting structure appear solid and grounded. Referencing the witch's gingerbread house in *Hansel and Gretel*, she striped some sections in alternating colors and aimed for a graduated spectrum in others. The house's interior, where lush tapestries and "gilt nonsense" are executed with "a dose of creepy humor," might, says O'Sullivan, derive from the handiwork of "Tony Duquette marrying Pee Wee Herman to produce a space that's part bordello and part Bollywood Regency fun house."

The first incarnation of Alessandro Mendini's Proust armchair was created in 1978 for the Palazzo dei Diamanti in Ferrara at a time when the designer saw modern design's strict principles giving way to ornamentation and symbolism. He reimagined a Rococo Revival fauteuil and painted it with pointillist brushstrokes he lifted from a Paul Signac painting as a fictional commission for the nineteenth-century writer Marcel Proust. "I pretend that design is literature," said Mendini. "I tend to make objects into stories." By contrast, the chair's 2009 Geometrica incarnation, above, with its dynamic explosion of color-blocked stripes, could have been commissioned by the Mad Hatter.

The tightly constricted stripes in Anthony Hartley's designs have the lighthearted looks of ribbon candy and, at the same time, the potential energy of a tightly wound spring. The furniture maker based in Yorkshire, who describes himself as a "jumped-up joiner," originally crafted this polychromatic signature piece, left, out of polished plywood as an homage to Frank Gehry's cardboard Wiggle chair but its striped version, Smith 2nd, is a nod to clothing designer Paul Smith. Each of Hartley's pieces has its own unique color sequence. Edna 1, right, is an oak cabinet with one multicolored, striped, plywood drawer.

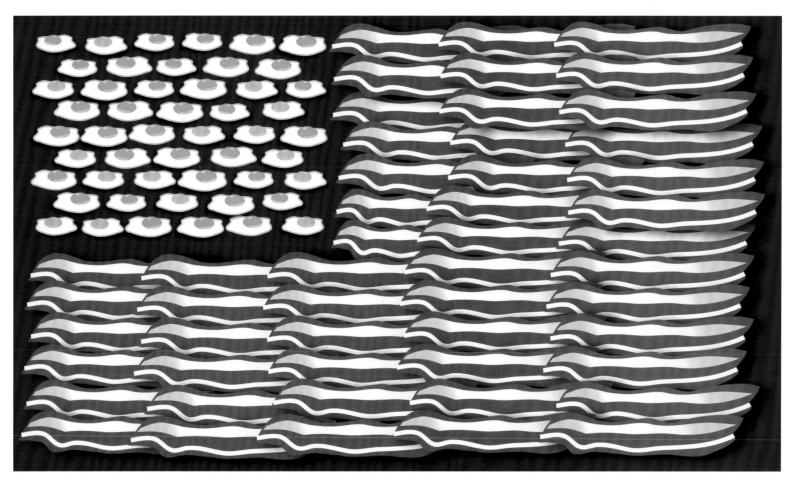

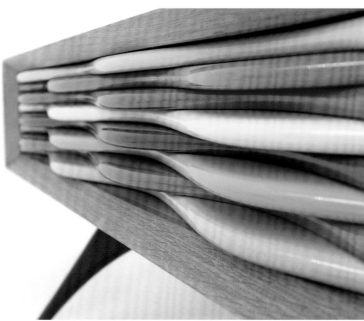

Fried eggs correspond to stars while rashers of bacon stand for stripes in *Diet for America*, a digital flag drawing created by Peter Rittmaster in 2009 as part of a series he cooked up on typical American meals that also features hot dogs, marshmallows, and French fries. "This piece acknowledges the sacred motif of the American flag," he says, "but it's also a visual statement about our country's over-consumption." In addition to artwork, Rittmaster has created everything from yachts to watches and he sees himself as a humorist, provocateur, and social commentator.

With its complex LED backlighting and hexagonal shape, Kasa Digitalia, the installation Karim Rashid designed for Abet Laminati at the Triennale di Milano Design Museum in 2008, resembles a life-size kaleidoscope. Conceived as a vehicle to showcase Rashid's collection of sixteen motifs, the striped, laser-cut laminate walls and floors folded on themselves into benches, tables, and chairs. Four-color inkjet printing patterns named Karimago, Myriad, Voxel, and Krit avoided any nostalgic connection to 1950s American diner laminate and situated these fresh versions firmly in the contemporary realm.

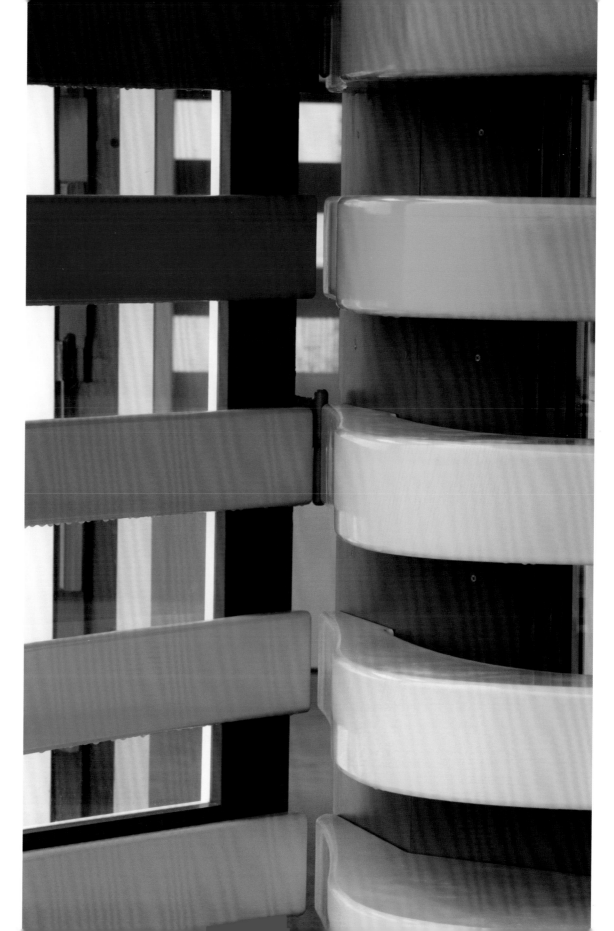

The first British beach huts with wheelchair and mobility scooter access were conceived by a:b:i:r architects and Peter Lewis of AEREA design and now line Boscombe Beach in Bournemouth, one of England's most popular coastal resorts. Entitled Seagull and the Windbreak, the project won an international competition that attracted 173 submissions and led to the district winning a 2010 Pier of the Year award. With dual-height kitchens and ramps that lead directly onto sandy beaches, the ergonomic structures redefine promenade architecture. Their yellow, green, and blue sheathing serves a practical purpose for the visually impaired while referencing beach umbrellas, sticks of rock candy, deck chairs, and a host of other striped vacation memorabilia.

In the world of design no name is more associated with stripes than Missoni. Since the 1960s the fashion house has incorporated stripes of every size and color into clothing, housewares, and eponymous hotels. For a 2008 commission by DuPont, designers Rosite and Luca Missoni visually wove together different colors of Corian to decorate conceptual living spaces at the Milan Furniture Fair. The single curved plane that forms the shower stall, with its seamless wall, ceiling, and floor, resembles striped fabric on a loom.

The improvised sequence of color, the irregular patterning, and the slightly off perspectives in the eight canvases that comprise Jochen Twelker's *The Excursion*, 1997–2000, can be seen as either threatening or cheerful. It currently occupies a hotel lobby in Amsterdam, but when it originally hung in its own room during a group show, the gang of truncated bodies it portrays appeared to vibrate and project an intrinsic tension and rhythm. Twelker customarily paints with wide streaks, thin stripes, rectangles, and circles and is content for the narrative in his work to emerge as a comment about the superficiality and subtext of clothing.

Resembling a large basket, the hanging Nest Chair Patricia Urquiola designed for Moroso's Tropicalia collection in 2008 is handmade from three plaited shades of thermoplastic polymer strands wrapped around a faceted tubular frame. Patrick Norguet's Rainbow Chair, on the other hand, is a feat of technology. Designed for Cappellini in 2000, its strips of multi-colored acrylic resin must be joined by ultrasound. "It's comparable to a Frank Stella painting," says curator Murray Moss, "but instead of a canvas depicting a spectrum of color, it's a chair."

The body of work produced by the self-taught California painter Karl Benjamin between 1950 and 1995 contains generations of stripes. Known for his use of saturated, sunny colors, the artist developed surfaces that avoid any allusions to depth and show no evidence of brushstrokes, as in #17, a painting from 1970. "No green in Benjamin alludes to foliage; no brown alludes to dirt in which the foliage grows," wrote critic Dave Hickey. "Benjamin takes these hues, burdened as they are with primal references and makes them back into free colors, live presences." Or as Benjamin once put it simply, "It's about getting the colors right."

In the foyer of a glamorous Fifth Avenue loft owned by Jamie Drake, left, a pair of Robsjohn-Gibbings stools flanks a vintage Intrex table that dates to the late 1960s. The Gene Davis silk-screened prints that occupy an entire wall are also of 1960s vintage. Drake used the collection as a departure point for the space's color palette; a base of deeply saturated magenta holds together a grouping of furniture from diverse periods. Davis wanted people to perceive his work three-dimensionally. "It's almost as if I were, in my stripe paintings," he said, "doing a spatial abstraction of time."

A 1971 Gene Davis print entitled *Alice Tully Hall Sampler*, referencing the soprano and cultural promoter, hangs in Mark McDonald's upstate New York gallery alongside an Ettore Sottsass table and a Michele de Lucchi vase, right. Davis often referred to a musical component in his work and felt his motif of choice, stripes, depicted rhythmic pauses. "Music is essentially time interval and I am interested in space interval," he once said.

Designers Carl D'Aquino and Francine Monaco are adept at injecting wit and color into interiors that feature serious, collectible furnishings. For their first collaboration with London-based Savoir Beds they created a stripy, fringed design in the belief that the bed should be celebrated as the joyful center of the bedroom.

Doug Meyer attributes the sense of play and irreverence he injects in his product and interior designs to his need for continuous stimulation. A pronounced use of horizontal and vertical lines imposes a subtextural grid that rallies together the jolts of color he often introduces. In the living room of a 1940s stucco house in Miami Shores, an overstuffed, kelly green Florence Knoll sofa converses with a pair of handsome Martin Eisler chairs as they sit on an evenly striped Doug & Gene Meyer rug. One wall is clothed in a graphic zebrawood veneer, another in an expansive, shimmering, ball-chain curtain, but their shared verticality imposes a rigidity that allows other colors to go wild. "Who wants to be serious?" he says.

PARADOX

Prolific inventor Dr. Yoshiro NakaMats—credited with holding a record 3,200 patents—has a three-part method for unleashing creativity. After he free-associates in a peaceful "static room" with calm, neutral walls, he cranks up music in a "dynamic room," with black-and-white-striped walls, and then holds his breath underwater while he jots down surfacing ideas on a Plexiglas tablet. To some people, listening to pulsating sounds while staring at a high-contrast surface is a sure recipe for a headache, but NakaMats believes the experience leaves him feeling sharper and more aware.

Architect and designer Josef Hoffmann made subtle black and white stripes, elemental distillations of ornamentation, a hallmark of his creations in the early twentieth century. His use of stylized stenciled wall stripes and gridded textiles was unprecedented. Dorothy Draper, the preeminent interior decorator of the 1930s and 1940s, also saw dynamic appeal in black and white stripes, routinely using their forms to energize nondescript hallways and inconsequential walls. She dramatized her Modern Baroque interiors with zebra carpeting and overscaled checkerboard floors— design gestures the trade still refers to as "Draperisms"—while her contemporaries considered

themselves brave for even daring to use occasional subtle black accents. These graphic devices may all reference the zebra-striped walls first discovered at villas in Pompeii—their inhabitants found that alternating lines of soot and lime proved to be quick, practical, economical decorating solutions.

Coco Chanel also named these two opposites among her favorite colors: "I have said that black has it all. White too. Their beauty is absolute. It is the perfect harmony." Chanel's preference showed in the little black dresses she wore with yards of pearls; in her classic, two-tone beige pumps with black-banded toe caps, still a mainstay of every Chanel collection; and in the black jacket lapels she trimmed with strips of white braid. When she launched her first perfume, No. 5, in 1921, the sobriety of its packaging—a white cardboard box edged with black piping—was strikingly similar to a funeral card, but Chanel's imprimatur lent it the elegance of a piano keyboard.

Economy rather than aesthetic concerns pushed Norman Joseph Woodland to team up black and white alternating stripes when he invented the barcode in the 1950s. He lengthened the dots and dashes of Morse code vertically until they formed a rectilinear grid and chose black because

38   it was more efficient to print
with than any other color. It also
absorbed light from a scanner
efficiently, and against white, the
most reflective color, it delivered
a clean, clear scan. Now attached
to every conceivable type of
merchandise in every part of the
globe, barcodes are a packaging designer's nightmare, a bean
counter's dream, and a universal
illustration of innovative black-
and-white thinking.

A woman in a bathing cap, far left, holding a horizontally striped awning fabric epitomizes the British, early-twentieth-century stance on beach modesty, which called for regulation black-and-white-striped coveralls. Scott Blake creates technologically savvy por-traits of everyone from Jane Fonda to Jesus in collages of individual bar codes that relate to their lives in some aspect, as well as bar code clocks, left, that operate as time-keeping screen savers. Italian architect Giò Ponti worked with stripes throughout his career. In the director's offices at the Società Ferrania in Rome, below, his 1936 design scheme recalls his love of an "exactness of an excess."

Finnish artist Esko Männikkö began his ongoing Harmony Sisters series in 2005. A portfolio of animal portraits taken in close-up, one image may cap-ture the swish of a horse's mane while another focuses on a cow's unblinking eye. His back view of a zebra, right, is arguably the most formally composed and painterly of the series. Even though Männikkö's image seems to suggest otherwise, embryological research reveals that a zebra's white stripes are actually additions to the animal's fundamentally black skin.

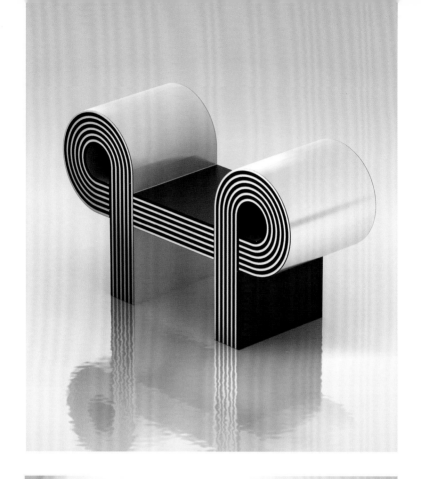

Most of the mathematically precise furniture and sculptures created by architect Marcello Morandini are executed in monochromes or in black and white. In his lacquered Posseduta bench, top, he forces black and white stripes to lend what he describes as an "active and surprising architecture to a traditionally passive object" and ends up with a seat that straddles the distinction between furniture, sculpture, and a three-dimensional logo.

Cap and Blazer, a carpet design from Interface, right, resembles an over-scaled line-up of striped English public school ties.

Sunlight streaming through skylights provides a blank wall in Arrop, Ricard Camarena's restaurant in a Gothic mansion in Valencia, Spain, with all the artwork it needs. Photographer Jessica Antola captured the elongated striped shadows as they tracked across the cellar space.

Filipino artist Geraldine Javier uses stripes as compositional elements in her work. "I have a tendency to put a lot of stuff in my paintings and stripes provide support, order and stability," she says. In her *Arrangement in Gray and Black*, a 2008 diptych, she reinterprets a black-and-white portrait Arnold Newman took of Diana Vreeland in 1974. By completely eliminating the style maven's head and expressive hands but leaving intact the shell of her striped djellaba, Javier created a memento mori.

Glenn Leitch's clever renovation of Playboy Enterprises' midtown Manhattan offices involves giant-scale branding. His shrinelike rendition of the legendary bunny head logo dominates the focal wall in a double-height atrium. By embedding it into a sea of black and white stripes, he introduced a formality and respectability that successfully reminds visitors that the company's interests extend further than its infamous men's magazine.

Whether hung vertically or horizontally, London interior designer Kelly Hoppen's boldly striped wallpaper designed for Graham & Brown is a timelessly neutral backdrop for furnishings of any period.

The bar code–based, black-and-white-striped walls architect James Biber created for chef Stephen Asprinio's restaurant, far left, serve many purposes: food orders are taken on an iPad, so Biber derives the décor from digital language, which also conveys a sense of "fast food" and "casual"; they direct the internal flow of foot traffic; each 20-foot-high panel enjoys high visibility from the street; and the stripes themselves are staggered at intervals that literally spell the restaurant's name, Pizza Vinoteca, when seen from a distance.

Tucked between small bars and neighborhood shops in the historic center of Madrid is a low-budget, affordable housing project, left, that won awards for its architects, Ciria + Alvarez Gomez. The three-story building contains seven living spaces, five garages, and a number of interior courtyards and terraces. Its sliding panels enable residents to modulate ventilation and shield large glass windows from the street commotion, and their striped motif is a contemporary reference to traditional Mediterranean window shutters. The black-and-white-striped facade at street level also discreetly integrates the building with the surrounding, predominantly horizontal architecture.

An exhibition about dazzle painting and ship camouflage inspired Patricia Van Lubeck to decorate her first car with a similar paint treatment, above. After two weeks and hundreds of rolls of masking tape, every inch of her 1975 hunter green Opal Kadett was covered in stripes—including its wheel openings. Other motorists loved and hated the car in equal measure; their general reluctance to come too close blessed her with expansive parking spots. She credits this first foray into car striping as the event that transformed her from a bookkeeper into an artist.

Over the course of his long career, German artist Gerhard Richter has painted many curtains, but he considers *Large Curtain*, 1967, to be his most successful for the calmness exuded by its light and dark vertical striping. A lack of visible hems or means of support moves the depiction of an everyday object into the realm of abstract art. This work prompted him to transition to a series of corrugated iron paintings. Richter dedicated the paintings in this series to the still life painter Giorgio Morandi, who rendered monumental portraits of humble, everyday objects in opaque gradations of gray. Richter was born in Dresden when it was still behind the Iron Curtain, so to him a drapery symbolizes a territorial demarcation between the visible and hidden or between the permissible and the forbidden. Here the stripes evoke cell bars or even striped prisoners' clothes. Many of Richter's paintings from the same period contained similarly undefined edges. "I blur to make everything equal, everything equally important and equally unimportant," he explained.

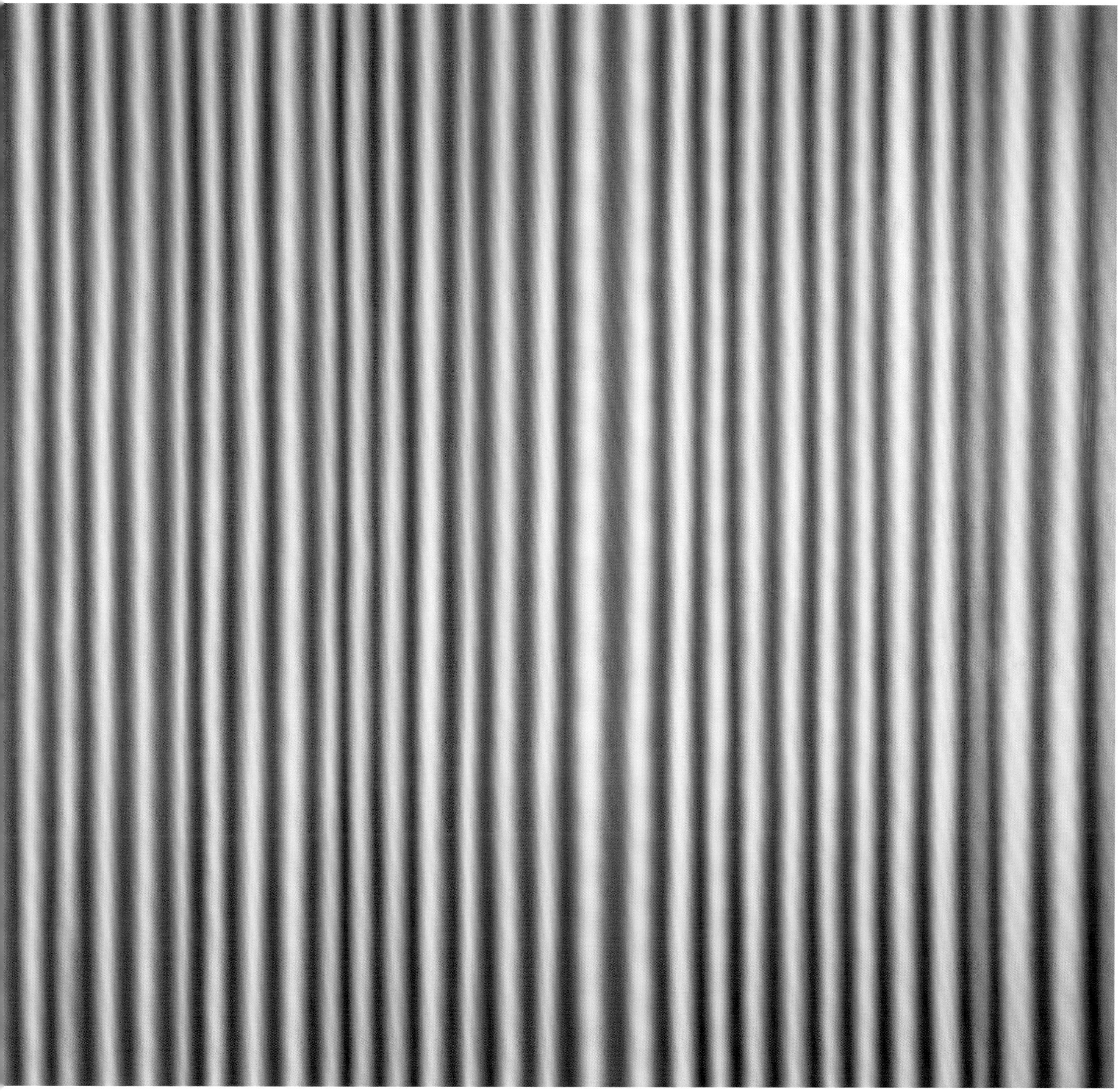

San Francisco designer Ken Fulk decided black and white stripes would be the most appropriate foil to a client's contemporary art collection, left; included is *Woman in Curlers* by Larry Sultan. The masculine pattern of the geometrically printed rug neutralizes the fussiness of the floral chairs. In another house, right, Fulk prevented a dominant fireplace from visually taking over a teenage girl's bedroom by striping its chimney to accentuate its height rather than its girth. Then, aided by Fornasetti pillows and wallpaper printed with a vine pattern, he introduced horizontal banding on side tables and upholstery to divert attention away from the corner.

Architect Donald Billinkoff surrounded a fireplace in the vestibule of a New York City brownstone, right, with freestanding slabs of linac marble; its pronounced linear veining accentuates the verticality of an adjacent two-story stair. The upright lines also impose a sense of order onto an asymmetric arrangement of furniture that includes a 7-foot-long embroidered leather bench, an elliptical rug by Suzanne Sharp for the Rug Company, and a framed photograph of a sweeping staircase from Michael Eastman's series on Cuba.

Award-winning Chicago designer Joan Craig settled on a primarily white palette for the master bedroom of a show house in a classic 1916 Lake Forest home, far right. Walls paneled in a striated silk by Ralph Lauren provide the room's only pattern and impose a calming, unifying effect for the room's other decorative objects including a large chandelier, a gothic fire screen in Lucite, and an ebonized Biedermeier chair. Black piping on the sofa's upholstery subtly introduces another horizontal line.

In a Manhattan apartment overlooking the Hudson River, above, French designer Patrick Naggar used black-, white-, and green-veined marble to build a master bathroom. Placing the grain parallel to the room's longest side makes the 200-square-foot space feel larger. Frosted mirror walls also erase boundaries and reflect the motif, so that, in certain light, the room appears to be entirely striped.

Clothing designer Geoffrey Beene often used his house in Diamond Head, Hawaii, as a halfway point when he flew from California to Japan. Black banding, lower left, saves a simple white staircase from obscurity and stripes in a bedroom, upper left, contrast pleasantly with framed views of lush vegetation and the ocean beyond. In the kitchen, far left, black and white stripes are a natural accompaniment to a decorative Polynesian frame. "The exterior architecture of the house was clean and sculptural," says editor Dara Caponigro, who produced a story there for *House Beautiful* magazine, "and the interior stripes mirrored that modernity."

To Sue Timney, stripes are the purest markings. She has based every textile collection and interior she has designed since the 1970s on them, relying on the motif to lend her projects a historical dimension and a modicum of illusion. In the drawing room of her house on the coast of Kent, stripes provide a modernist, op art slant. The white-on-white collection of ceramics on the fireplace sits below a print of novelist Marsha Hunt made by Timney's husband, Justin de Vinneneuve. On the room's other side, Timney-Fowler wallpaper frames a silk painting and relates to the clock carpet she designed for the Rug Company.

Medical training at Tulane University endowed Geoffrey Beene with a keen awareness of female anatomy, but he always viewed clothing design as an architectural challenge. "You are faced with a piece of crepe or wool, the flattest thing in the world," he said, "and you have to mold it to the shape you want." His experiments with lines and stripes on suits and evening gowns are his graphic legacy. Throughout his career he consistently used black and white, and often isolated or highlighted individual stripes. A double-faced, buffalo wool plaid shrug with bias horsehair insets, from 2002, demonstrates his perception of the body as one continuous plane. A cotton sweater and cotton faille skirt with a stripe of appliqué grosgrain, from spring 2003, illustrates how even a single, well-placed stripe can serve as ample ornamentation.

Overleaf: Conceptual artist Vanessa Beecroft is known for creating *tableaux vivants* of scantily clad women that blur the lines between theater, social commentary, fashion, and art. Terms generally applied to her work, such as ferocious, authoritarian, Spartan, sexually provocative, and passive aggressive also describe *Ponti Sisters*. This 50-minute-long dual-projection video installation documents two statuesque women as they walk stiffly into a room and lie down on a sofa. The room, furniture, and women's bodies are dressed in nothing but wide stripes.

The unreinforced, coffered dome and the oculus of the Pantheon inspired Eric Cohler to design a circular bathroom for Kohler, in Wisconsin, left. Alternating horizontal bands of Ann Saks off-white and dark gray limestone tiles exaggerate and aggrandize the 6-foot-wide shower stall, and high-perched windows flood its interior with natural light.

Stripes cover the entire facade of the Wynwood Building, left below, a behemoth of a 45,000-square-foot commercial structure that occupies an entire block in downtown Miami. "Dazzle ships" from World War I inspired property owner Tony Goldman and architect Rafael de Cárdenas, of the New York firm Architecture at Large, who mapped out the exterior's motif. "It's rare to encounter op art on such a monumental scale," says photographer Daniel Aubry. "The effect is kinetic; an assault on the optical nerves. This is especially true when the building is viewed from one of its corner angles and all those black and white lines seem to recede to infinity."

A graphic and historic connection exists between the striped churches and cathedrals found across Europe and the striped mosques characteristic of Northern Africa. In both areas, stripes exaggerate the scale of the already monumental buildings and distinguish them from the surrounding architecture. In the Church of San Giovanni Battista in Ticino, Italy, right, Mario Botta designed alternating stripes of dark gray Riveo granite and white Peccia marble. "As you draw closer to the interior center and approach the altar," says architect Chip Bohl, "the stripes intensify and become three-dimensional, as if to amplify the 'otherness' of the space. The surface is no longer flat . . . the optical and religious transformations could go hand-in-hand."

When Lobmeyr first issued Josef Hoffmann's exquisitely regimented Series B drinking set, in 1914, the manufacturing process was extremely labor intensive: fine pinstripes were lacquered onto lead-free glass after it was coated with enamel paint, then acid was applied to melt the nonlacquered sections. Today Lobmeyr covers the entire glass with acid first, to achieve a matte finish, and paints on the enamel stripes afterward. "The more refined a glass becomes, the more one might appreciate its contents," says Rhett Butler, who carries the line in his New York store, E. R. Butler.

Daniel Buren's first public work, *Two Levels*, was installed in the forecourt of the Palais Royale in Paris in 1986. It resembles a giant board game or the truncated remains of a candy-striped Greek temple. The artist based his design on a grid and dispersed 260 concrete columns throughout the courtyard in a pattern that mirrors the geometry of the surrounding colonnade. In the original scheme, the columns were reflected

in channels of running water but the Minister of Culture, who sponsored the work—and ironically has an office on the site—let those components fall into disrepair. Buren does not consider stripes to be the subject of his work; he sees them as a means to recalibrate the way visitors see another object or scene. The installation initially received a mixed reception, but is now a favorite haunt for skateboarders and portrait-seeking tourists.

TRIBAL

With roots firmly planted in the regalia of war and heraldry, striped clothing and insignia historically united some people and segregated others. They instill pride or impose shame, enforce hierarchy or celebrate individuality. The mere fold, thickness, and position of a toga's stripe, for example, maintained the class structure of ancient Rome by differentiating an average citizen from a senator or an equestrian.

According to historian Michel Pastoureau, in the eighteenth century the language of stripes became particularly nuanced. Certain stripes were designed to be worn only by peasants, others by aristocrats; some were for daily use, still others for holidays. Stripes also began to appear on household items meant to be hygienic, such as underclothes. Every stripe served a clear and universally acknowledged purpose in households throughout Europe.

Striped neckwear, a later iteration, signifies clannish camaraderie and team spirit even today. The first recorded club tie dates to 1880, when members of Oxford University's rowing team ripped the striped bands off their caps and tied them around their necks. Decades later Fred Astaire made a fashion statement by repurposing his Brooks Brothers Repp Tie—the name is a corruption of the garment's "ribs," which run perpendicular to the selvage—and belted it around his waist.

Eventually stripes migrated away from mere decorative edges and into clothing's main cloth. The first striped vests were known to have enlivened the uniforms of dapper valets and butlers in Victorian England, but the origin of pin-striped business suits is murky. Design director Steven Willis eloquently pegged them as a sartorial declaration of reliability and probity that echoes the "columns in an accountant's ledgers," but they are more likely related to sporty boating suits from the 1890s. Decidedly dandy, the popularity of these white-striped outfits peaked in the 1920s, when they served as informal alternatives to the customary staid, dark attire available to men in that era. To this day, the wearer of a pin-striped suit strives to be perceived as an upright citizen, although, as Paul Theroux has said, "In countries where all the crooked politicians wear pin-striped suits, the best people are bare-assed."

The official Breton T-shirt, a boat-necked top with twenty-one navy stripes that each correspond to a Napoleonic victory, became standard issue for French sailors in 1858. After a trip to the seaside in the 1930s, Coco Chanel appropriated it, paired it with baggy matelot pants, and the utilitarian shirt suddenly became unisex and chic. Thereafter it became symbolic of a freewheeling bohemianism that still appeals to men and women of every age and nationality. The gondoliers' top shares the Breton's nautical heritage but more likely owes its design to a need for high visibility, an inoffensive pattern, and a knack for appearing both formal and informal—all invaluable attributes of any chauffeur's uniform.

Plaid is, of course, an advanced evolution of lone stripes. Quilters mix them with ease, but only the stylishly heroic can carry off an outfit that combines both stripes and plaids. The Duke of Windsor did it with notable flair, and designers Jean Paul Gaultier and Vivienne Westwood aren't intimidated by such extreme pattern coupling. Neither, apparently, was Albert Einstein, who said, "Once you can accept the universe as matter expanding into nothing that is something, wearing stripes with plaid comes easy."

Double-breasted, wide-lapelled, pin-striped suits have as much appeal today as they did when leading man Gary Cooper, top, sported them in the 1940s. Pinstripes earn their name from pinhead-sized dots of yarn woven into worsted wool to produce a broken line; parallel rows of two or more pinheads form what are known as "lace-line stripes," and "rope stripes" have a pronounced diagonal. The thickest pinstripes mimic tailors' chalk markings—produced by a particular milling process that renders the lines purposefully smudgy. Whatever the stripe's thickness, it is always meant to emphasize the suit's cut. No one theory satisfyingly accounts for the coloration of the red, white, and blue helical stripes on a barber's pole, above, but the red stripes are often associated with the medieval practice of bloodletting, a service barbers in that era also provided. The relaxation of Britain's moral code in the early twentieth century allowed bathers to reveal gradually more skin, left, but stripes more than any other pattern were associated with hygiene and decency for decades after swimsuits were first introduced in the 1830s.

Dark wood paneling helps Alberto Pinto establish a clublike atmosphere for a home office in a Marrakesh villa. Striped wallpaper modernizes the lexicon of heavy ornamentation that includes wrought-iron window screens, cloisonné doors, an Oriental carpet, and a fret-work chandelier to save the space from becoming a Moorish cliché.

A repetitive use of horizontal lines effectively grounds a dining area by Australian designer David Hicks within an open-plan apartment overlooking Melbourne Bay. Heavily grained sea-grass wallpaper sets off the gridlike image in a photograph taken by the owner, a textured rug from Hicks's Cadyrs collection anchors the floor, and jaunty stripes on a Kenzo fabric energize antique Louis XVI armchairs.

Antique dealer Tom Blake subconsciously surrounds himself with stripes. In his upstate New York house one closet is filled with neat piles of striped blankets from the 1940s; another reveals a phalanx of vintage striped neckties; bookshelves are lined with dime-store novels stored page-out to reveal their pale red and green edges; and then there are stacked spools of multicolored masking tapes and military insignia, above left. Blake's affinity for stripes spills over into his artwork, such as a sculpture, below left, where strips of weathered wood are applied to a wavy-edged 1950s curio shelf unearthed at an estate sale, left. "There's no logic to it," he says, explaining his predilection's early roots, "but when I was a kid growing up in Texas, those hot summer nights felt a lot cooler when I was sleeping between striped sheets."

In an Upper West Side Manhattan pied-à-terre, right, workshop/apd firmly grounded a lounge area with a subtext of stripes in order to elevate the space's ceiling optically. The Bouroullec Brothers' Facet armchairs flank an accordion-fronted credenza by Matthew Fairbank that's vertically akin to Warren Platner's steel wire ottoman and a mixed media, multistriped painting by Nola Zirin.

The bucolically situated Hamptons farmhouse Joanna Bobrowicz shares with her husband, Chas Godson, contains a diverse selection of furnishings that look to stripes to achieve a degree of harmony. In the hallway, left, a vividly striped stair runner pulls together an antique Japanese lacquer cabinet, a seventeenth-century English table, a papier-mache umbrella stand, a beaded pair of Victorian needlepoint footstools, and a nineteenth-century model ship.

The determined color scheme in the entry hall of a stately English home is saved from stuffiness and predictability with the introduction of a Carnival carpet by Paul Smith for the Rug Company; its patterning abstracts the pink dado panel that winds around the room's perimeter. The randomness of the motif diffuses the formality introduced by the arrangement of the chairs and oil painting and lends lightness to the greens of the wall and brocade upholstery.

Jim Thompson's Bamboozle textile, above, recalls bamboo plants and Chinese calligraphy, but its overscaled pattern can also be perceived as disjointed vertical stripes; this dual character qualifies it for use in a variety of applications.

Most of the rooms in this spacious 3,500-square-foot Central Park West apartment designed by D'Aquino Monaco, right, are full of dynamic color and a spirited mix of twentieth-century Italian and French antiques, Lucite sculptures, and edgy artwork. By way of contrast, a subtle underlay of stripes on a silk carpet creates a clublike atmosphere in the master bedroom, where walls wear chocolate-brown wool.

Jay Jeffers takes the formality out of a collection of fine antiques in a living room, right, by upholstering an oversized ottoman with Pierre Frey's Alhambra fabric. "Because the pattern is confined to the stripes," he says, "there's a whimsicality and the space feels edited." The serious/whimsy theme also extends to the room's focal point, a classically composed still life by Jeanne Duval, a New Hampshire painter whose art career began once she decided to replicate the famous paintings often reproduced on sugar packets.

Irish artist Sean Scully began painting stripes in 1969, and they have been a recurring motif in his work ever since. Regardless of their colors, his stripes, lines, bands, and crossbars are purposefully devoid of narrative, meaning, or subtext; he intends for this to endow his work with a universal appeal and relevance. "If I ever adopted another motif," he says, "that would mean I have exhausted the potential of the stripe. And I haven't." The blocks of color and stripes in *Square Light 2*, a 1988 aquatint, are, to his mind, simply a testament to "the difficulty and possibility of coming together." Scully connects his vocabulary of stripes to an early affinity for checkered-looking Irish fields and the Moroccan djellabas and patched circus tents he encountered on his travels.

The strong horizontal lines in Leo Adams's living/dining room resemble the intricate stonework of an Italian villa, but are created from pickled and stained strips of plywood. Like practically every object in his house near Yakima, Washington, they were reclaimed, recycled, or rescued from a landfill. The core of the house is built around his grandfather's cabin, which Adams relocated onto 40 acres on Ahtanum Ridge amid a grove of Russian olive trees and banks of sage. The artist invests as much time and creative energy into decorating his house as he does painting landscapes, and horizontal lines are integral to both.

For the dining room in her own 4,000-square-foot eclectic modern house in Costa Mesa, California, interior designer Melissa Palazzo based the scheme on a favorite item—zebra-printed cowhides. The table and leather chairs are from her company, Pal + Smith; Lars Bolander designed the raffia stool.

When Benjamin Noriega-Ortiz transformed a SoHo, New York, penthouse into a bachelor pad for rock star Lenny Kravitz, he assigned the cavernous space a white shell and a dark floor; then he proceeded to carefully introduce defiant, antique furnishings to create a sophisticated-but-fun vibe, such as an ornate frame that houses a portrait of Jimi Hendrix. A Lucite swing begged for a central location, so the designer accentuated its potential path of trajectory with a striped zebra rug, an object no longer associated only with trophy rooms and hunting lodges.

Stripes figure prominently in the design of the majority of the world's flags, and national pride has also always played a role in the philosophy behind Vivienne Westwood's clothing designs—she either refers to it reverentially, venerating English tailoring and tartans, or rebels against it, as she did in the Punk era. Here, she let a faded glory flag inspire needlepoint pillows.

Irish-born designer Luke Irwin literally dreamed up his silk Doves and Stripes rug. One night as he fell asleep he visualized the top-heavy canton in the American flag and saw its stars morphing into doves taking flight. When the design was rendered tangible in silk and wool and hand knotted using a Nepalese weave, the Irish nation presented it to President Obama.

London-based designers Nipa Doshi and Jonathan Levien celebrate story-telling and cultural harmony in their work, and were inspired to create their Principessa daybed by Hans Christian Andersen's classic fairy tale *The Princess and the Pea*. Many thin mattress layers of Jacquard weave and toile de Jouy combine to form a textile mille-feuille.

During the restoration of an Upper East Side Manhattan townhouse for a couple with four children, interior design firm D'Aquino Monaco patched together twenty-seven different patterns of wallpaper along the entire length of the staircase. The selection is a seemingly random mix of contemporary, Arts and Crafts, and Victorian designs, but it actually establishes the color palettes for the rooms that lead directly off the landings and hallways. The living room, for example, wears a base coat of pear green stucco and its windows are framed with plum taffeta curtains.

The Nubian people displaced by the construction of the Aswan Dam brought traditional decorative painting techniques with them to their new homes across the Egyptian desert; familiar motifs on the doors and gates helped the settlers feel grounded again. Deidi von Schaewen's photographs, left and lower right, reveal these striped emblems, some of which have been in continuous use since 3,000 B.C. No two doors are ever the same. A door von Schaewen photographed in Tunisia, upper right, similarly conveys its owners' personality. Both African cultures use stripes to indicate status and lend a sense of ceremony to entranceways.

After a visit to Dakar, furniture manufacturer Patricia Moroso set up a workshop staffed with Senegalese and Malian craftsmen who were living in Italy and invited designers, including Patricia Urquiola, to design a range of furnishings. The artisans use traditional, stripe-based patterns that have been passed down from generation to generation of weavers, resulting in items like the Reii bench, top. In every culture, striped textiles have their own particular narrative. The value of this rectangular, early-twentieth-century Burmese silk sarong, above center, relates to the intensity of labor needed to create it: two artisans working together send hundreds of small shuttles back and forth through a warp of over 1500 threads to create an interlocking cable weave. A colony of Muslims expelled from Andalusia wove the striped silk fragment, near right, in Tunisia; a Moorish influence is evident in its tilelike design and Fatima hand details. The nineteenth-century cotton textile, center right, with polychrome horizontal stripes, was made in Turkey or Syria for the European market. The construction of the nineteenth-century Persian Jajim, far right, is based on a floating warp technique that produces a lightweight silk weave; this fabric is often used as a saddle cover, blanket, floor covering, or wall hanging.

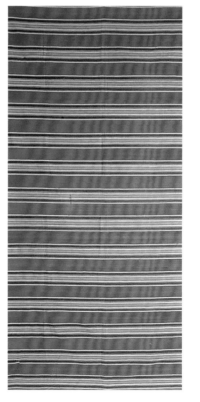

A complex wrap resist technique—whereby a single, long piece of cloth is folded into accordion pleats and wrapped at precise intervals before tie-dying—was used to create this Lahara turban cloth. Made in Rajasthan, India, in the 1860s, its fifty-seven pattern changes and twenty different zigzag motifs were achieved with fugitive dyes, meaning it has been painstakingly redyed whenever faded to ensure its survival as a family heirloom.

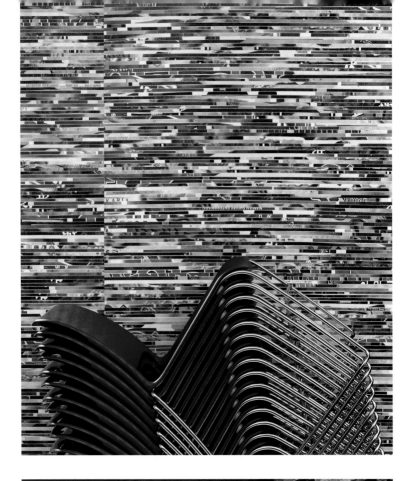

Lori Weiztner creates her Cinema Posters wall covering, above, from recycled Bollywood movie posters collected in bulk, shredded into thin strips, then woven by hand onto a nylon warp. The end result is a colorful mosaic that has a subtext of drama, romance, and action at its core.

Architect Glenn Leitch incorporates many branding devices into his design of Playboy Enterprises' midtown Manhattan offices, right. The pièce de résistance is a wall constructed from thousands of back issues of *Playboy*. Fifteen thousand magazines were stacked into sets of twenty-five, each magazine's ¼-inch spine was stapled into place in the stack, and every stack was set into a 14-inch-tall steel box to achieve stability on the 8.5-by-12-foot-high wall. "It obviates the need for signage in the reception area," he says.

David Rockwell designed Jaleo, a restaurant headed by chef José Andrés, for the Cosmopolitan luxury resort in the heart of Las Vegas. Its private dining space, right, looks like a surreal library, thanks to walls and a ceiling lined in custom-designed paper that simulates shelves crammed full with books. The striped surface infuses the low-ceilinged space with a sense of optical depth.

DIRECTIO

"It's the nature of stripes to make things move," says painter Markus Linnenbrink, "they squeeze distractions out of space." A striped repeat of a single color on a canvas, object, or wall automatically triggers the eye to search for a dominant or central focal point when in fact none may exist. Multicolored stripes, on the other hand, animate as their pigment levels and values spar with each other so that one stripe appears to float in front of or shift behind its neighbor. Painter Josef Albers talked about our ability to hear a single tone but inability to see a single color. That is, we connect it to its neighbor or another hue; this explanation captures the essence of what happens visually when a host of striped motifs appears to be, as he says, "in continuous flux."

The potential energy housed in a single stripe is particularly potent when it becomes associated with an object that actually moves or travels. An infinity stripe streaked along the side of a putt-putt train's carriages, for example, makes us wonder if it's a TGV; similarly, a thick diagonal stripe stenciled onto a warplane's fuselage makes it look intimidating to enemies in combat.

The streamlined style that evolved out of the Depression Modern style of the 1920s and 1930s resulted in sleek, aerodynamic styling on everything from radios to ocean liners. At the time, it represented progress and visually reinforced the belief that modern life, signified by extended, unbroken stripes, was fast-tracking its way to the future.

Today's shiny vertical surfaces of an office building or the massive plate glass windows of a department store double as massive sidewalk mirrors that reflect an abstracted portrait of city life. They showcase streaked impressions of cars and elongated lines that correspond to a throng of pedestrians as if they were billboards advertising motion.

Similarly, the striped logos on the sides of many prominent brands of sneakers are meant to convey action, and are of course prime branding real estate. These motifs connect the wearer to a lineage of racing champions and romanticize even the most banal of sports. Any generic white lace-up can turn the wearer into a sprinter or soccer star with the addition of Nike's swoosh, Adidas's three-striped trefoil logo, Puma's Form Stripe, or Onitsuka's Tiger Stripe.

Choreographers from Nijinsky to Bob Fosse also knew how to harness the kinetic properties of stripes on apparel to make dance costumes enhance movement. "Executed correctly a stripe on stage lengthens the line of an arm or leg and that, in turn, extends the dynamic of any artistic movement," says legendary costumier William Ivey Long. His stripes exaggerate a villainous curve or underplay a comely, big-boned physique.

Stripes are commonly thought to visually elongate the body by drawing an observer's eye up and down when, as Hermann von Helmholtz showed, the opposite is true. The nineteenth-century physician proved definitively that a square composed of horizontal stripes appears taller and thinner than an identically sized square composed of vertical stripes. "Those rules about side-to-side stripes adding girth are not hard and fast," continues Long, "because a body isn't static. It's never a still, contoured piece of architecture, and when it encounters the geometry of a rigid stripe there's a visual collision."

Ali Cavanaugh's painting *Falling Through Your Redolence*, top, captures a mind's-eye image of her daughter in a blissful jump. "Stripes create a visual rhythm like no other pattern," she says. Coco Chanel dressed the Ballets Russes dancers, center, in tasteful, striped, knitted wool when she designed the bathing and tennis suits for Serge Diaghilev's Paris production of *Le Train Bleu* in 1924. The fabric panels of hot air balloons, left, are often striped; their alternating colors help earthbound spectators track their paths across the sky.

Jörg Sasse wants viewers to impose their own narrative on his *Striped Plane* photograph, right. His manipulated 2010 image incorporates a found snapshot of either a model or actual plane—inconclusive—that's either in motion or stationary—also inconclusive—and could be out of focus, ascending, or falling. Aeronautical buff Eliot D. Hawkins remembers similar stripes exactly as they appeared on planes used during the D-Day attack in 1944: "broad black and white stripes at the wing roots, and fuselage ahead of the tail assembly so they could be easily identified by the allied gunners on the ground."

The overall shape and exaggerated, looping curves of Tord Boontje's Shadowy chair, top, evoke the light-weight, striped beach furniture popular in the 1920s, and appear to instill movement in what is a static object.

In the design of his prototype room divider, Phenomena, left, Korean-born designer Sang Hoon Kim pieces together layers of ash ribs and bends the wood so it appears to meander like flowing water. The screen's horizontal struts break up its fixed mass and cast stripy shadows as they interact with changing light throughout the day.

Venetian-born architect/designer Gaetano Pesce's furniture is heavily conceptual. He conceived his Up 5 chair and Up 6 ottoman, right, in 1969 as political commentary: dressed in uphol-stery that references prison stripes, the chair's voluptuous female curves and the ottoman chained to it refer to "the shackles that keep women subjugated."

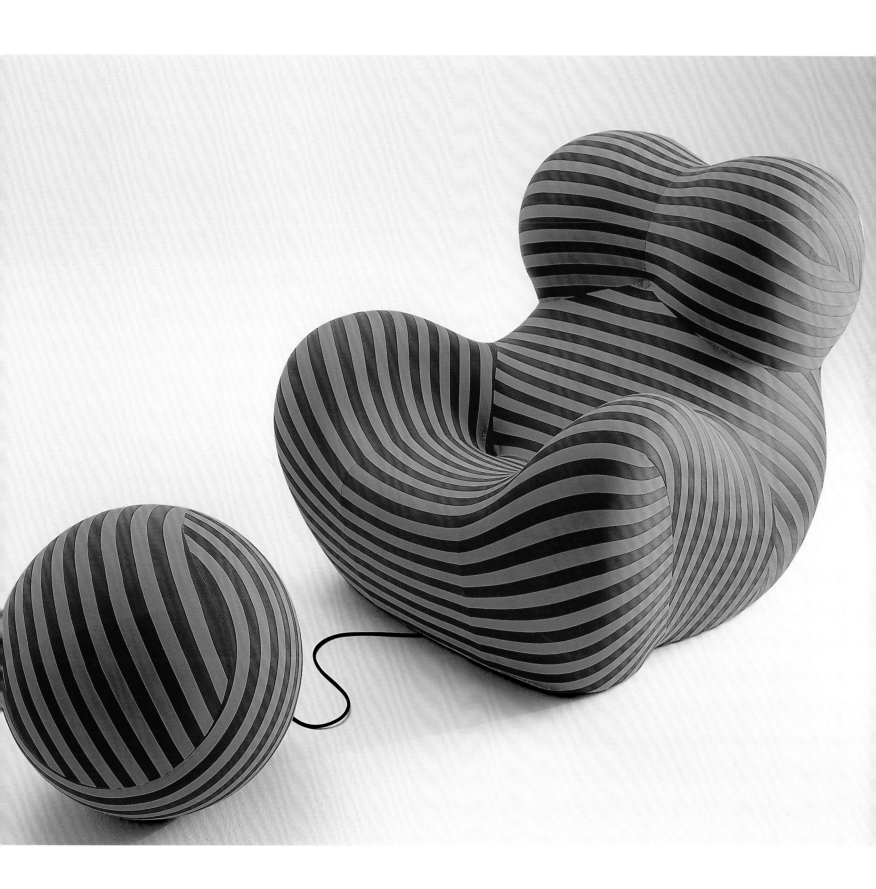

In 2011 German artist
Markus Linnenbrink created
DIEDRITTEDIMENSION, left, a
permanent installation at the
Justizvollzugsanstalt prison in
Dusseldorf Rath. He converted
a 130-foot-long tunnel into a
three-dimensional, striped painting where the colors on the ceiling
and floor progressively widen, drip,
change hue, and offer inmates'
visitors an unconstrained experience of total color emersion. In his
BUILDINGSTEAMWITHAGRAINOFSALT,
above, the artist added one layer
of colored epoxy to the form each
day; it therefore serves as a testament to the length of time it took
him to construct the sculptural
shape during 2010 and 2011.

Resembling a giant, cubic musical stave, British artist Liam Gillick's first outdoor sculpture in the U.S., NINTEENFORTYSIXXISYTROFNEETNIN, 2004, is a minimalist, powder-coated aluminum structure. Many of his colorful pieces are meant to parallel nature, so this location in the middle of a meadow garden on the grounds of the Aspen Art Museum feels apropos.

For his 2009 design of the Wright restaurant inside New York's Guggenheim, architect Andre Kikoski evokes the movement of the iconic spiral Frank Lloyd Wright created for the museum with a curving, layered wall treatment and ceiling that echo the museum's overall shape and exaggerate the room's perspective. Liam Gillick developed a site-specific installation for the room, *The horizon produced by a factory once it had stopped producing views*, an expansive sculpture constructed from extruded yellow and orange aluminum bands that encases parts of the walls and ceiling and crowns a sweeping banquette.

StudioMDA treats stripes as energizing guideposts at ExerBlast, right, a family-friendly workout facility in New York that houses a jungle gym, climbing wall, and obstacle course.

In a sleepy town in the Velez-Rubio district of Southern Spain, ELAP architects designed a day care center, top, from a child's perspective, and designated stripes as a central motif for the common area. Ribbons of green, orange, and blue create a stimulating, lively atmosphere.

The Children's Library Discovery Center, right, at the Queens Central Library in Jamaica, New York, is the only public library in the U.S. to incorporate interactive science exhibits. Lee H. Skolnick Architecture & Design Partnership employed colorful signage and stripes to lead children through various programming spaces.

Designer Jonathan Adler always pursues fun in decorating. In the Greenwich Village apartment he shares with his partner, Simon Doonan, both the ping-pong room and the dining room started as simple, stark white shells with soaring ceilings, but Adler has transformed them into brilliant performance stages for strategically placed mid-twentieth-century furnishings, edgy artwork, and dollops of kitsch. Hand-loomed zigzag carpets play a pivotal role in conveying his underlying philosophy: neither life nor tchotchkes should be taken too seriously.

As part of her Human Zoo series, photographer Matilda Temperley assembled seven naked women in her London studio, covered their bodies with black and white body paint, then captured them on film as they danced, gyrated, and channeled zebras. Temperley—who gave up a profession as a tropical disease scientist to pursue photography—is inspired by the physicality of dancers and circus performers.

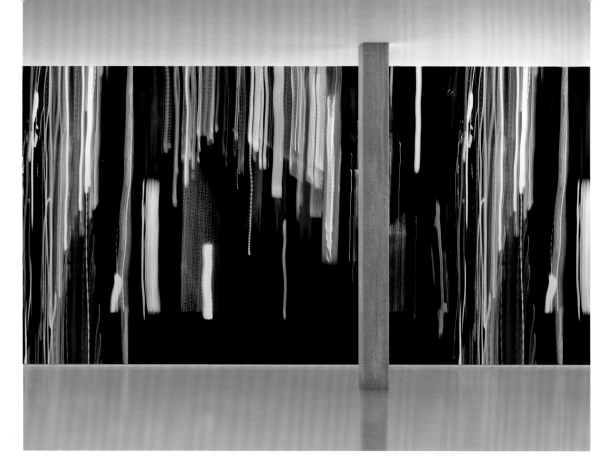

Slow Exposure Stripe is a digital collage of several views along Brick Lane—a lively street in London's East End—taken by fashion designer Paul Smith for a project commissioned by Maharam. As the camera's shutter speed is manipulated, the street and traffic lights are transformed into vibrant, animated brush strokes. The uneditioned piece is printed digitally in 40-inch-wide panels on a paper substrate, and has been permanently installed in seven locations; Smith created six additional digital projects for the textile manufacturer.

The Hotel Everland, a 2007 installation on the roof of the Palais de Tokyo in Paris, was conceived by artists Sabina Lang and Daniel Baumann, who work together as L/B. The temporary structure served as a functioning hotel, but each guest could stay a maximum of one night. All the interior surfaces inside the 365-square-foot structure are rounded and smooth, and the streamlined exterior is wrapped with a three-tone stripe that implies motion, though of course none exists.

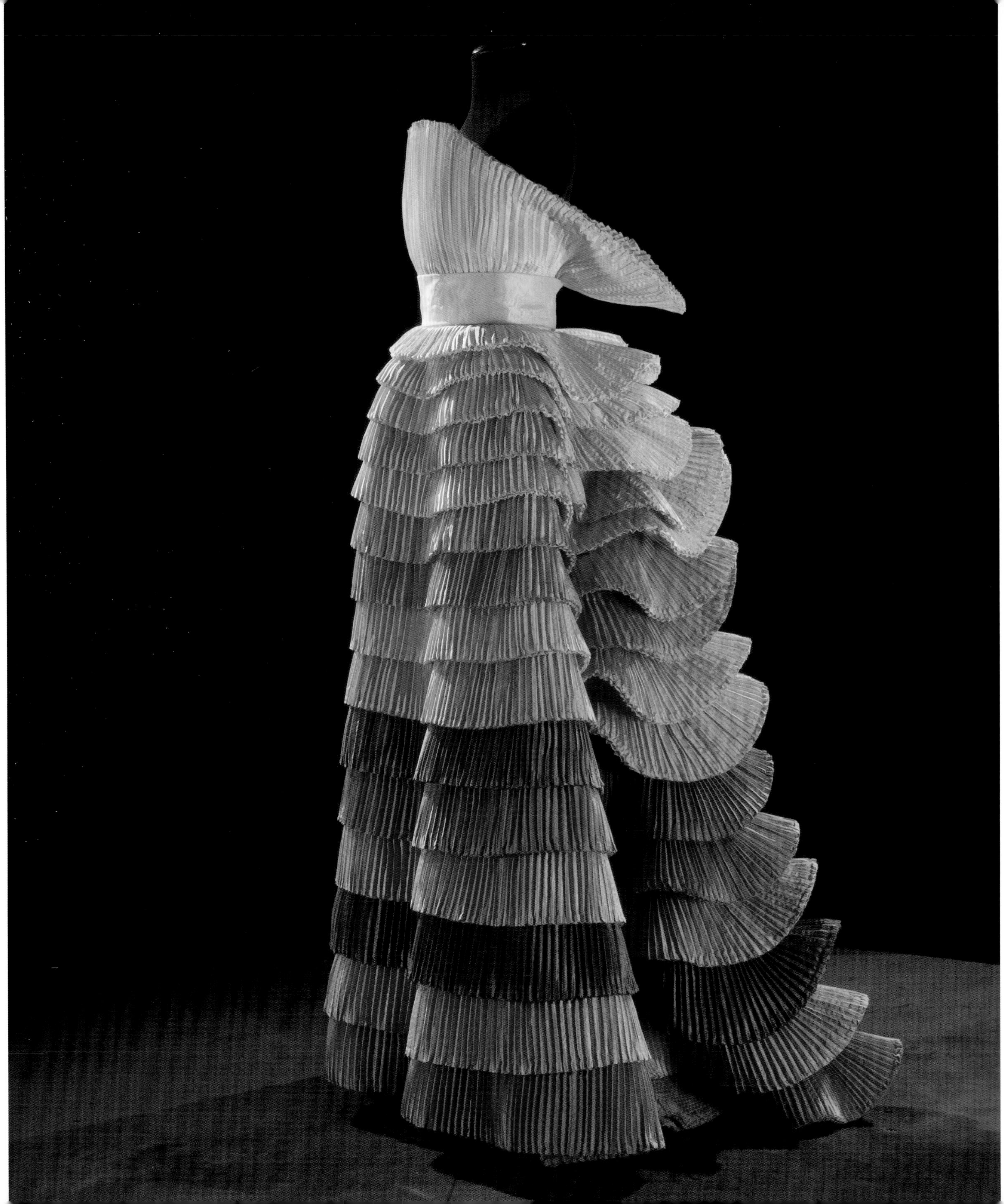

Art and fashion are synonymous in the works of Italian designer Roberto Capucci. One of Italy's most creative couturiers, he has based gowns' silhouettes on peeled oranges, calla lilies, fire, and butterflies. He may make an entire ensemble out of silk ribbons, glow-in-the-dark rosary beads, or garden pebbles. The iconic rainbow-colored gown he designed in 1992 from pleated silk taffeta, left, resembles ruffled origami.

The woven fabric of United Nude's Fold bootee wraps around the foot like a stripy turban or scarf, above. The designers—Rem D. Koolhaas, nephew of the famed architect, and Galahad Clark, of the Clarks shoe dynasty—conceived the upper and heel as a continuous display of fluid movement.

English painter Ian Davenport either pours household paint onto fiberboard, then tilts it to make it run certain directions, or injects colors onto a canvas with syringes. His finished, striped canvases don't merely imply movement, they actually represent the pull of gravity on pigment. In *Citric Etching*, right, one of an edition of thirty works from a 2011 series, his stripes literally leave a strong impression.

The use of colorful stripes as a metaphor for movement is amplified on a flight of stairs in interior designer Muriel Brandolini's tiny weekend guesthouse overlooking Peconic Bay, on New York's Long Island, above. She turned a flaw into a feature by applying a random assortment of rainbow-colored paints to the risers of an enclosed staircase, imbuing the space with a tropical feel.

The design team at SPG Architects covered three flights of stairs in an early-nineteenth-century, four-story townhouse in Brooklyn Heights, New York, right, with Paul Smith's Swirl carpeting from the Rug Company as a way to liaise detailed traditional architecture with contemporary furnishings and an eclectic art collection. "The varying widths and sinuous nature of the stripes mediate the gentle curve of the stair in a way that a truly orthogonal stripe wouldn't have done," says partner Coty Sidnam. "Because there is something riverine about the way a brownstone stairway bends and flows down through a house, perhaps unexpectedly, it isn't disorienting to descend."

Paul Smith's Swirl carpet, right, has a grounding effect that imparts human scale to a cavernous room; it helps mediate the proportions of a low-hanging, oversized chandelier and squat desk.

According to Paris-based photographer Deidi von Schaewen, the outlying streets of Cairo contain more cars with covers than any other part of the world. Documenting them is one of her ongoing projects: some are abandoned due to mechanical problems or simply because their owners ran out of gas money. Tarpaulins are sewn in neighborhood workshops or customized by a car's owner, creating a wide variety of designs. The stripes always run horizontally, however, in the hopes they'll trick passersby into perceiving a degree of motion in the stationary vehicles.

Overleaf: Judith Turner began taking photographs of large-scale buildings forty years ago. Her 2005 series of New York City skyscrapers is named Liquid Architecture because, depending on camera placement, the monumental, solid structures can often appear molten. Reflections in the glass curtain walls that sheath them convert air traffic, cloud formations, and soaring birds into parallel striations of color and light. Through Turner's lenses, buildings merge, melt, and drip ambiguously, like murals in motion or giant textiles with mutable warps and wefts.

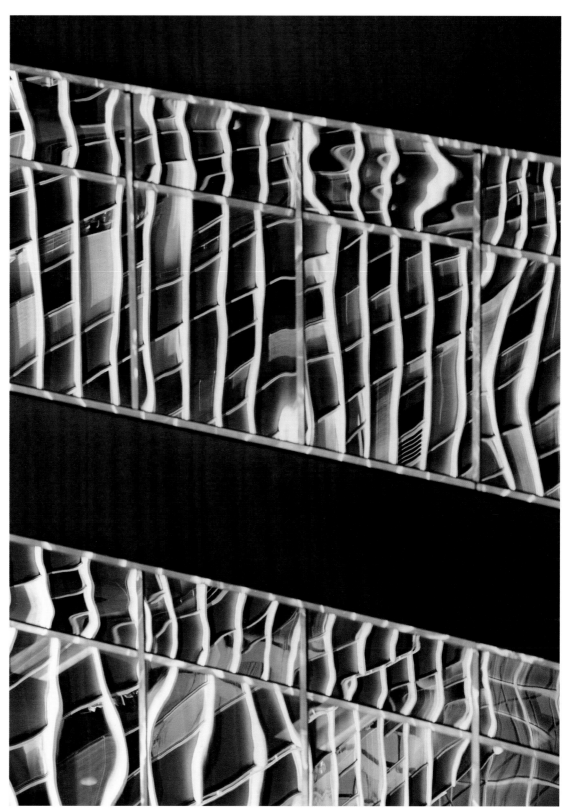

OPTICAL

An artistic formation of stripes that intentionally explores the nature of vision ranks as a retinal titillation. Maybe it cajoles the eye into perceiving invisible colors that have no fixed beginning or end, or maybe it assaults and fatigues the eye into registering spasmodic after-images. Any such type of visual dilemma serves as a metaphor for unease or uncertainty.

Illusions were foundational to the work of op artists in the mid-1950s and 1960s, and stripes, which lend themselves so well to creating unexpected visual distortions, became a primary medium. Some critics accuse artists including Victor Vasarely and Carlos Cruz-Diez of perpetrating hostile attacks on the senses because their dizzying canvases and light projections incorporate false perspectives and perpetrate color deceptions where lines appear to swell, warp, or vibrate. Of the many proven optical tricks developed, moiré arguably stands out as one of the simplest and most effective. It involves overlaying two lined motifs at an angle to form an interference pattern where the intersection points of the superimposed lines appear to break or widen in an unfathomable way.

Disruptive patterning evolved in the animal world as a particularly clever and useful type of visual deception. Zebras rely on

their markings to cause chaos. For example, when a lion views several zebras from a distance, their stripes intermingle until it can't tell a snout from a flank. As long as it is incapable of deciphering where one body starts and another ends, it can't strategize an attack based on luring a single zebra away from the herd. To make matters worse from a predator's point of view, visual hell ensues when a pack of zebras disperses.

This tactic has also been adopted for human use. It's clearly impossible to hide a battleship at sea, so the premise of disruptive camouflage was used effectively to convert World War I vessels into graphic billboards. The U.S. army enlisted landscape painters to decorate commandeered ocean liners with crosshatching and zigzag stripes in order to confuse the enemy. At sea, the ships resembled floating cubist paintings, and Picasso therefore took all the credit for the concept. When viewed from a plane or through a gunner's range finder, these bold blue, black, and white asymmetrical markings made it impossible for the enemy to calculate a ship's speed, direction, size, or model. In short, they effectively sabotaged any potential strategy of attack.

Inspired by a Bridget Riley painting, art dealer Pearl Lam

commissioned craftsman Bruno Romette to paint a nondescript two-story stair in her otherwise psychedelically baroque London townhouse with a similarly intricate design of large circles broken down into stripes. Romette used miles of masking tape and acrylic paint with a high pigment density to execute a swirling, black-and-white op art design. The 20-foot-high space is now a monumental homage to dazzle painting, disruptive camouflage, and interference patterning. In direct contradiction to earlier theories about how optical illusions affect mood, however, Lam's stairwell manages to exude a peaceful, calming air.

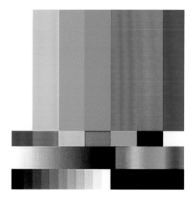

Serious op art painters from the 1960s frowned upon clothing fashion accessories, like sunglasses, left, that capitalized on the movement's popularity. In television's early days, before round-the-clock broadcasts, cameramen used stripy test cards to calibrate the alignment, chroma, and tint bars, below left, that appeared to announce the beginning and end of daily programming. British painter and naval officer Norman Wilkinson developed "dazzle paining" in 1917 to camouflage ships used in World War I.

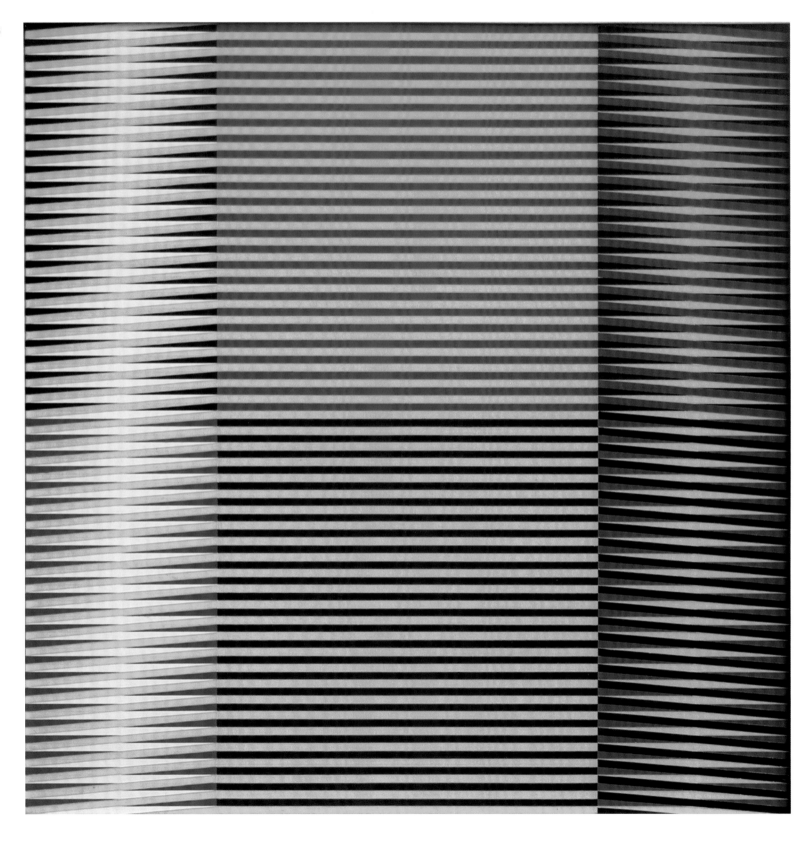

Venezuelan artist Carlos Cruz-Diez's experiments with color, lines, perception, and sensation preceded the op art movement of the 1960s, which exploits the fallibility of the human eye. He is regarded as the grandmaster of optically kinetic art. His work gradually evolved from abstract to highly geometric, and he sees color as an unstable, mutable entity. His ephemeral constructions explore how art and the color that radiates from it are separate. *Induction Chromatique 59*, 1973, left, plays with the phenomenon of afterimaging, when the retina continues to perceive one color's complementary hue after the gaze is averted. *Transchromie 1965/2007*, right, is based on the behavior of color when viewed through overlapping, translucent Plexiglas strips. "The line is not an absolutely aesthetic element; it is an element of efficacy," he says, "an essential and unadorned element, unique, to show the metamorphosis, the transformation of color."

Overleaf: Illustrator Jeroen Koolhaas and art director Dre Urhahn, of the design firm Haas & Hahn, want their ongoing development, O Morro—The Hill—to become the community-driven art installation with the most participation in history. For the project's first phase the team developed a complex striped design for the facades of thirty-four buildings located in the central square at the entrance to the Santa Marta favelas in the heart of Rio de Janeiro, and employed local inhabitants to spend a month painting it. The formerly dismal 7,000-square-meter hillside shantytown has now become an inspirational landmark.

The Nebuta House, a museum dedicated to a unique form of Japanese storytelling that involves giant paper lanterns and thousands of lights, was designed by Vancouver, British Columbia–based firm molo. The result of a competition judged by architects Jean Nouvel and Tadao Ando, it stands on the waterfront harbor in the northern city of Aomori. Over 800 40-foot-tall steel ribbons make the facade look, from certain angles, something like a giant red car wash. Elongated shadows from the light that filters through also stripe the walls and floor of the building's all-black interior.

The complex, asymmetric Bridging Tea House, designed by Mexican architect Fernando Romero, rests next to a pond in Jinhua City, Beijing. It is often mistaken for a three-dimensional maze. One of its main features, a wide expanse of steps built from matte red concrete, is Romero's modern interpretation of a traditional Chinese garden bridge.

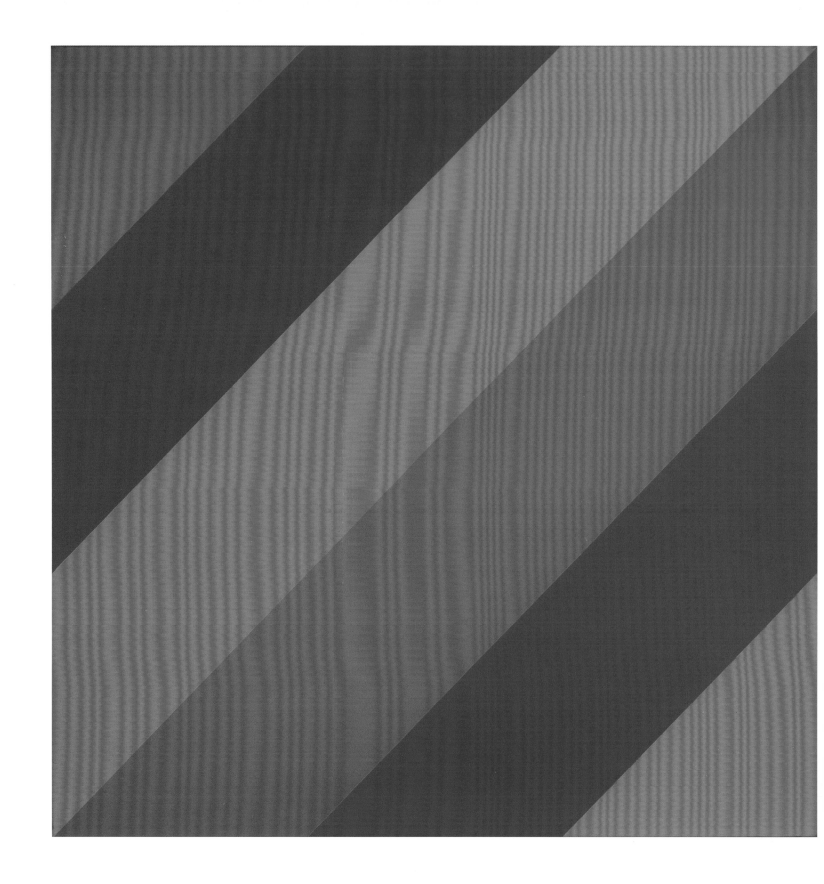

Karl Benjamin stopped painting in 1995, making his pieces much sought after by collectors. He vows that he never consciously set out to create optical illusions, even when covering a canvas with diagonal stripes, as in *#10*, from 1975. "These forms could be seen advancing or receding," he says. "They could have a three-dimensional effect despite the fact that when I painted them, I was thinking flatness—diagonals and the flatness of the canvas." His color choices are similarly visceral: "I wasn't trying to achieve maximal optical bounce; it wasn't a case of making mechanical choices in terms of which color would vibrate the most against another—a machine could have worked that out better."

In a spacious Manhattan apartment, interior designer Carl D'Aquino and architect Francine Monaco installed a predominantly red library in response to a client's desire for a room that would contrast strongly with the adjacent blue living room. Striped opaque panels on scarlet Roman shades cover an entire wall of windows and alternately hide and reveal panoramic views of Central Park.

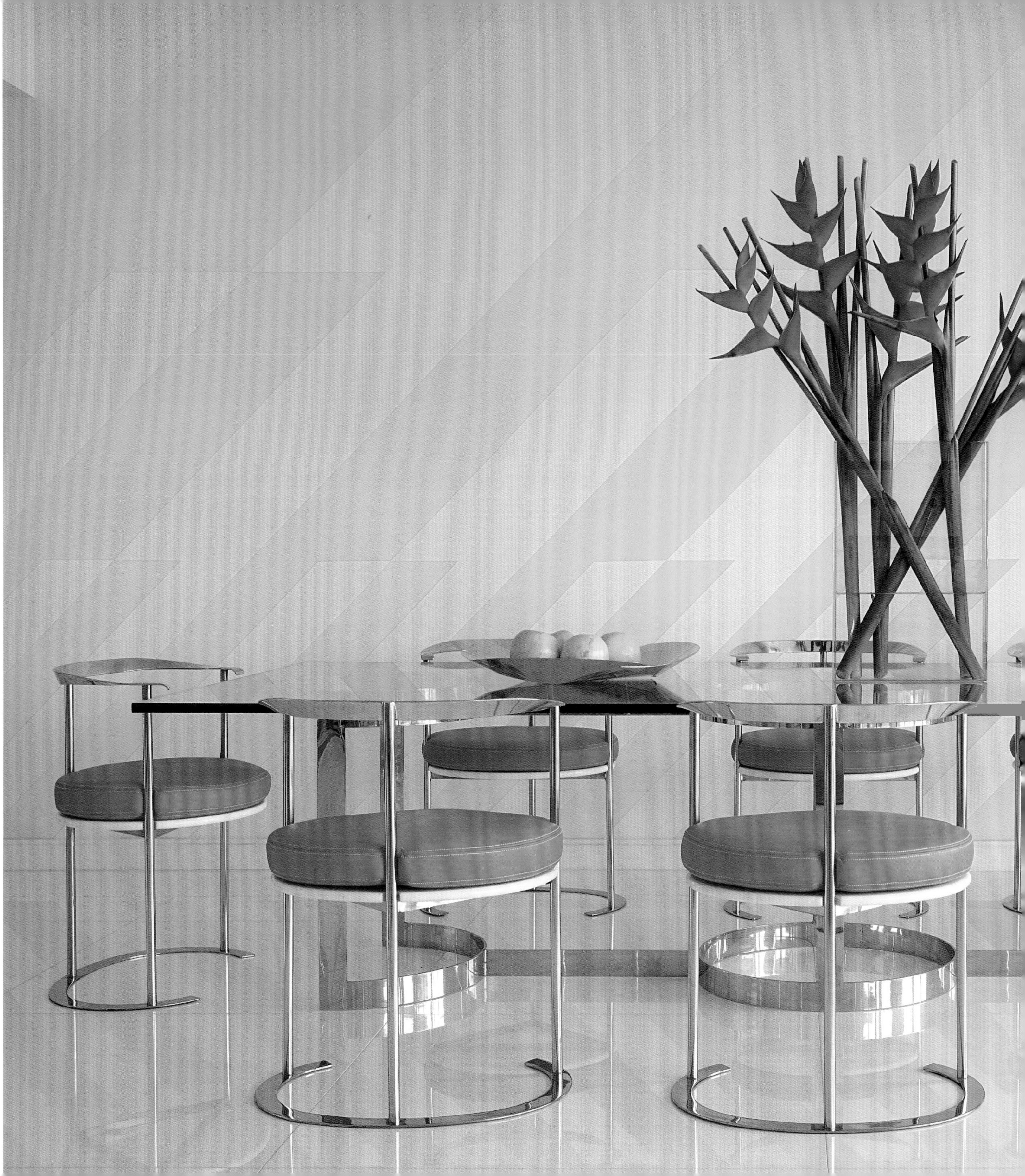

Orange is the reigning color in the
Miami duplex Tony Baratta occupies
on weekends. It appears in the form
of vinyl on the living room walls, fabric
in the powder room, and in the upholstery of the Luigi Caccia Dominioni
chairs in the dining room, where the
focal wall perpetuates the citrus
theme. A canary-yellow mural based
on an Alexander Girard graphic and
painted by Adam Lowenbein covers
the 9-foot-high walls with stripes in
thicknesses that range between
5 and 20 inches. Its lightning bolt
lines are also reflected in the floor's
white glass tiles.

When CBT architects renovated the 125,000-square-foot offices of Boston law firm Brown Rudnick, they carved a double-height atrium out of two floors to transform a formerly mundane reception area into a grand entrance. They further dramatized the space's loftiness by commissioning a Sol LeWitt mural, *Wall Drawing 833 Black and White Wavy Bands*, 1997, and amplified its visibility by strategically positioning reflective surfaces—the glass walls of a conference room, a Warren Platner coffee table—to bounce snippets of its undulating stripes throughout the space.

While reviewing a series of photographs she'd taken in a zoo, German photographer Andrea Wilken experienced a twinge of sadness at the thought of a magnificent zebra behind bars. She personally couldn't repatriate the animal—but technology could—so she manipulated her image and placed the zebra on his namesake crossing, as if he is walking back home to the Serengeti.

Overleaf: Admired for the purity and the integrity of her artistic vision, Agnes Martin is known for the subtle horizontal and vertical lines she painted onto pale, washed backgrounds. Her geometric abstractions *Journey 1*, 1966, left, and *Praise*, 1976, right, are minimalist in form but contemplative and spiritual in nature, prompting one critic to see them as a "religious utterance, almost a form of prayer." Martin intended for her art to exemplify psychic calm, stability, and long-lasting beauty. Much of the delicacy of her canvases stems from the slight flaws in the lines—the evidence of her hand. "People who look at my painting say that it makes them happy, like the feeling when you wake up in the morning," she said, "and happiness is the goal, isn't it?"

Picnic a. martin '66

praise – a. martin

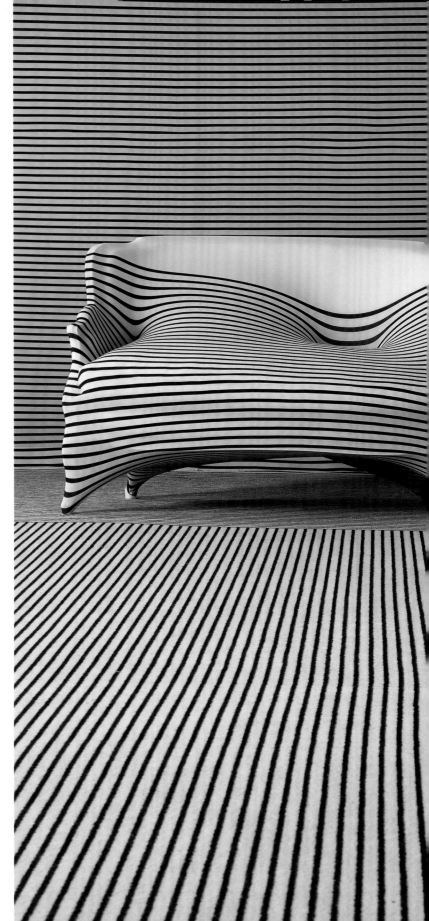

Glow, a 30-minute video essay by Gideon Obarzanek and Frieder Weiss, uses striped shadows as a sleight-of-hand device to make a dancer, above, appear to mutate in and out of human form.

In collaboration with Dutch designer Jurgen Bey, fashion designer Jean Paul Gaultier cocooned Roche Bobois furniture—a sofa and bergère—inside flexible striped lycra, right, for a surreal, severely lined room commissioned by *Elle Décoration* magazine in 2004. Gaultier's space references marine stripes and corsets, two of his archetypal clothing elements, as well as Jean Cocteau, who was once described as "a poet wrapped inside a painter wrapped inside a filmmaker." For his 1996 spring/summer ready-to-wear collection, Gaultier superimposes the ghostly outline of a voluptuous female body, in the form of black stripes of various densities, onto a masculine, loose-fitting pantsuit, far right.

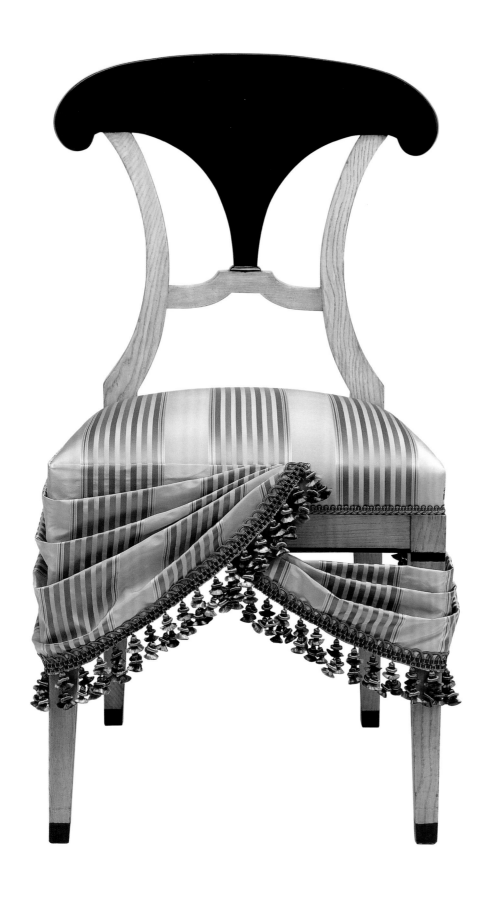

With its string of Houlès fringe tassels and swag of Beacon Hill Fresco fabric, Taillardat's conservative Biedermeier-style chair is ready to moonlight at the Moulin Rouge.

When Nan Swid and Addie Powell
created their housewares collection in
the 1980s, they included designs by
a group of stellar architects such as
Swiss husband-and-wife team Robert
Haussmann and Trix Haussmann-Högl,
whose portfolio contains everything from
utensils to buildings. The couple's mani-
festo is to produce "ad-hoc, irregular,
heterogeneously formalistic, ironically
illusionistic designs." Their 1990 jewelry
box, right, cut from sterling silver and
pear wood, wears a trompe l'œil clois-
soné draped scarf; the moiré transfer
on their Black and White Stripes buffet
plate, above, turns a ceramic circle into
a shimmering swatch of silk.

Artist Jim Lambie, a former Glasgow musician, now fills rooms with vibrant rhythms that are decidedly rock 'n' roll. Using all ten colorways of standard 3M industrial vinyl tape, the artist turns plain, unfurnished spaces into complex, high-energy mazes and grids. Floor plans always dictate his work's dimensions and direction, as in his 2010 installation at the Goss Michael Foundation in Dallas, Texas, left, where stripes move from the room's outer perimeter to the center in rigid, right-angled paths. Each length of tape overlaps the next by 2 millimeters so the overall floor is as seamless as if it were poured directly from a can of paint.

A complex system of layering makes the facade of the Brandhorst Museum in Munich, right and above, oscillate and, at times, appear to dematerialize like an op art canvas. Its architects, Berlin-based Sauerbruch Hutton, achieved the effect by placing horizontal strata of sheet metal underneath 36,000 vertical ceramic rods. When viewed in close proximity, the facade's twenty-three colors appear as a sea of shimmering stripes, but, from a distance, they merge into neutrality, an effect that's apropos for the home of a spirited collection of contemporary art.

In the Château des Ducs d'Épernon,
a historic estate south of Bordeaux,
Daniel Buren turned an enfilade of
doorways into a visually ambiguous
promenade in 1985. The themes of
doorways, frames, and contrasting color
processions are of perpetual fascination
to Buren. "The colors that we actually
experience," he says, "the subjective
sensations of redness and blueness are
arbitrary labels that our brains tie to
light of different wavelengths."

In 2008 Daniel Buren dipped into the
400,000-image-archive of photo souve-
nirs from his travels and art installa-
tions to create a series of inkjet printed
scarves for Hermès. Cropped doorways
and windows with striped borders
pay geometric homage to the fashion
house's iconic silk square.

PHOTOGRAPHIER AU CARRÉ
PETRES COLORÉES À TRAVAIL IN SITU
(DÉTAIL)
SÉOUL, CORÉE 11.12.06
HERMÈS ÉDITEUR - PIÈCE UNIQUE

The designs Maija Isola created for Marimekko from 1949 onward often involved the outlines of recognizable plants, leaves, and twigs. The large abstract patterns she sketched, right—30 meters long, to run the entire length of the company's printing table—also relate back to nature, however. The Silkkikuikka, or great crested grebe pattern, from 1961, mimics the flight path of a diving bird, and is still in production today on the company's sheets and tablecloths.

Bridget Riley produced black-and-white paintings in the early 1960s that explored the dynamic effects of optical phenomena. "I wanted the space between the picture plane and the spectator to be active," she says. "It was in that space, paradoxically, the painting 'took place.'" *Fall*, a work from 1963, far right, forces a dissonance between the part of the brain that knows the canvas to be flat and the part that wants to interpret it as a curved surface.

For an ambitious public project the MAK Center for Art and Architecture commissioned twenty-one artists to reclaim a space blighted by urban advertising. Susan Silton's resulting *If I Say So* billboard, left, hovered above the Los Angeles skyline for a period of two months in 2010. Her work typically combines photography, video, and offset printing and the blurred, distorted effects that mimic motion are often interpreted as a search for stasis. The piece is based on the phrase famously uttered by Robert Rauschenberg when he sent a telegram to a gallery to stand in as a piece of art.

In response to a commission by *Wallpaper** magazine, London designers Kiwi & Pom created the one-off Disco chair, top. Its 200 linear meters of energy-efficient, electroluminescent wire light up into a neon rainbow and even pulse when it's switched on.

For a student cafeteria at Applemore Technology College, a secondary school in Southampton, England, London architects SHH turn a riddle of disjointed rooms into a comfortable dining hall by introducing wide diagonal stripes on the walls and floors, left, to impose order, expose sight lines, and maintain the original building's semi-industrial vibe.

Many artists couldn't see the point of Daniel Buren's 1971 plan to divide the Guggenheim's iconic atrium into two equal parts with a suspended, 65-by-32-foot blue-and-white-striped banner, and pressured curators into literally folding his first large-scale, site-specific show the day before it opened. Donald Judd notably dismissed Buren as a "Parisian wallpaper hanger." He waited over thirty years, then successfully proposed another plan to transform the museum's venerated rotunda. *The Eye of the Storm*, 2005, incorporated an 80-foot-high paneled mirror, left, that bisected the space, giving visitors the impression that the seven-story circular ramp shimmied and dissolved into its own reflection. Buren also attached green tape in his signature 3.4-inch-wide strips as a border along the full length of the ramp's balustrade and applied alternating magenta stripes to panes in the skylight, right.

Due to an abundance of windows and a corresponding lack of wall space, Christopher Coleman designated the floors as the best location for art in this Miami Beach condo, left. He drew on his graphic design roots to create an abstract plan based around furniture configurations and asked a terrazzo fabricator who customarily works in airports to take his first residential commission. The resulting stripes and zigzags in the breakfast room are surprisingly calming. "They guide you through the space," says Coleman.

The first collaboration Jee Levin and Randall Buck of design firm Trove had with Knoll Textiles resulted in Sway, left, a wall covering that evolved out of a series of gestural, tactile paintings. Within the confines of graphic vertical tracks washes of color intermingle, flare up, and fade away as they constantly play with the viewer's perspective.

Design firm Barber Osgerby created five limited-edition Iris tables for the British firm Established & Sons in 2011. Machine-cut strips of solid aluminum embedded with anodized color form the circular bases, which are each fitted with a round piece of glass for a top. The graduated color choices are inspired by paint wands, textile swatch books, and catalogs of printing inks that display color ranges in sequential, subtle variations of hues and tones.

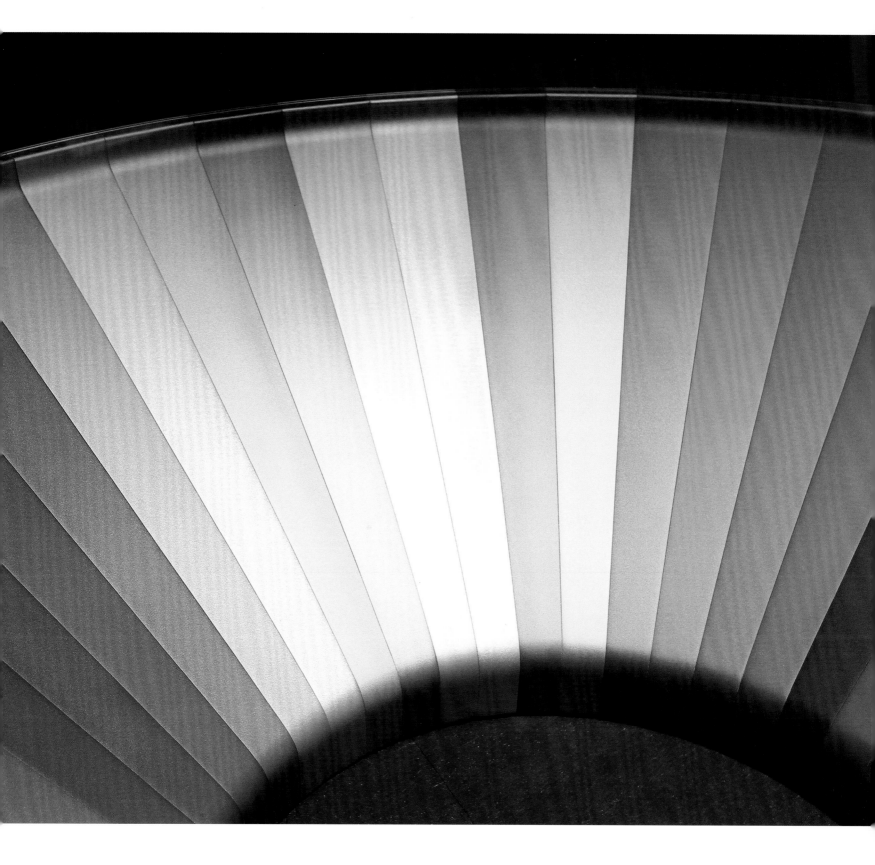

Just as a warp needs a weft, a vertical stripe is only strong when grounded by a perpendicular counterpart. Any upright line represents a resistance to the earth's natural pull of gravity; and poets have notably celebrated how columns so gracefully join their roof lines.

An upright line also symbolizes humankind's aspirations and the search for a better self. As writer Elie Wiesel said, "In philosophy you go horizontally while in mysticism you go vertically." Lofty proportions have been built into churches, cathedrals, and mosques of every persuasion for centuries to inspire, awe, transcend human scale, and direct the spirit toward heaven.

In interior design, vertical lines perform magic tricks. They perceptibly elevate ceilings and, as they direct the gaze upward, they widen the overall vista and make an interior spatially easier to grasp. But the sorcery ends abruptly when stripes are called upon to attempt to straighten a crooked or slanting wall—that they simply cannot do.

Due to their erect, dignified demeanor, vertically striped walls suit rooms where a degree of dignity is apropos. In moderation they radiate an air of authority, permanence, and masculinity. When stripes or columns flank an object or a piece of furniture they aggrandize it, leading one architect to refer to them as "design sentinels," but when that device is overused a stripe's formality can translate as confinement, stiffness, or immobility.

When maximalist fashion editor and curator Diana Vreeland commissioned Billy Baldwin to decorate her now-seminal Park Avenue apartment in 1955, he upholstered the living room walls and windows with a Gastón y Daniela scarlet chintz festooned with brilliant Persian flowers. In sharp contrast, he covered the adjacent dining area with floor-to-ceiling green, red, purple, and yellow stripes that also enveloped an entire banquette and several pillows. The floral/stripe combination fulfilled Vreeland's original mandate that Baldwin should create "a garden, but a garden in hell," and it's easy to imagine Vreeland enthusiastically saying "I never met a stripe I didn't like."

Painters also know intimately how plumb lines can affect any visual composition. "The vertical is in my spirit," said Henri Matisse. "It helps me to define precisely the direction of lines, and in quick sketches I never indicate a curve, that of a branch in a landscape for example, without being aware of its relationship to the vertical." Barnett Newman devised a vertical "zip" stripe motif that runs the full height of his canvases; it represents the viewer and replaces the traditional earth/sky dynamic with an envelope of color. In addition to anchoring a canvas, painters use vertical stripes to convey a sense of the frenetic. Cary Smith, whose work employs many geometric shapes, says, "The only way I have found to replicate the obsessive energy of the modern world is by painting vertical stripes of the same thickness."

New York City–based studio potter Kathy Erteman uses three-dimensional-looking slips and vertical stripes in textural glazes to ground the wide mouths of her wheel-thrown stoneware bucket vessels, left. For the final show of her Master of Arts program at London's Royal College of Art, in 1979, designer Sue Timney, below left, presented an animated film, *Stripy Sue*, where vertical stripes are used in an all-encompassing way to animate her body and surroundings. Punch and Judy puppet shows are mainstays of British seaside culture, and have roots that date to the sixteenth-century Commedia dell'Arte. The short, combative performances are traditionally staged inside a vertically striped, easily transportable booth, below.

148

In a 750-square-foot Paris apartment located between the Palais Royal and the Louvre, vertical stripes on a lounge wall modernize a 1950s parquet floor. Owners Simon Pillard and Philippe Rosetti executed the floor-to-ceiling treatment in paint rather than wallpaper to achieve a less-manufactured look that sits well with a graphic collection of wares by designers including Ettore Sottsass, Piet Boon, and Jaime Hayon.

In the living room of a Spanish Colonial Revival house James Lumsden designed in Hollywood, stripes play a key role. The room's ceilings range from 10 to 14 feet in height and adjacent spaces have ceilings that climb to 24 feet. Lumsden installed overlapping rugs with wide stripes to keep the lofty spaces grounded. "Their geometry emphasizes every curve I place in their proximity," he says.

Despite its deep associations with green, Ireland's official color is actually blue. When it comes to front doors, the country has a particularly extroverted, colorful vernacular tradition: here a homeowner in County Cork invents a heraldic scheme by combining patriotic stripes with the colors of a local soccer team.

Clannish customized wallpaper brings a sense of monumentality to an architecturally generic kitchen in Christopher Coleman's 1,150-square-foot loft in Williamsburg, New York. Black-fronted cabinets and black velvet wall-to-wall carpeting also help to emphasize the generous ceiling height.

In a stately late-nineteenth-century mansion that commands an enviable view in Tuxedo Park, New York, design firm D'Aquino Monaco hand painted alternating stripes over traditional boiserie and crown molding—on all four walls of its spacious living room. "There's a momentous entrance to this space, so it felt imposing and self-important," says Carl D'Aquino. "The stripes made it more compatible with our clients' upbeat personalities and the informal way they live. It's very graphic but it's also pale and subtle," he continues, "so before people recognize the color progression, they read it as sunlight."

Designer Benjamin Noriega-Ortiz challenged himself to create an adult, non-girlie, pink bedroom in his Rockaway Beach weekend house in Queens, New York, above. He saturated the walls with Benjamin Moore's Country Pink paint and installed matching translucent curtains with plentiful vertical folds to visually rectify an off-kilter back wall. A dyed Mongolian lamb bedspread, sheets imported from Paris, and an off-center La Murrina chandelier complete the monochromatic scheme.

Doug and Gene Meyer's painterly design aesthetic means their Crossroad rug, right, would look as good hanging on a wall as it does covering a floor. Their Tiki Pop rug, far right, also holds its own as a piece of art in a room where works by Nick Lamia (left) and Antonio Murado (right) hang on a wall covered in stripes composed of individual sheets of letter-sized colored paper.

Deidi von Schaewen's around-the-world portfolio of striped structural walls includes one spotted in Southern India, above left.

Flowers and foliage inspired the color scheme of a long driveway wall Topher Delaney incorporated into a San Francisco landscaping project, left. Using Fine Paints of Europe high gloss for its weatherproof qualities and dense colloidal mix of pigment, the designer created twenty-three stripes in nineteen custom colors. Their variable widths abstract the color fields of a cutting garden nearby.

Architects Glass Kramer Loebbert striped the facade of a storage facility, right, on a Berlin campus vertically and in four shades to offset the two-story building's proportional stockiness. "The pattern also references barcodes and may be understood as a colorful interpretation of the four nucleotides that inform the module of all life," says Johannes Loebbert. The interior doesn't need to be exposed to daylight per se, but the translucent industrial glazing nevertheless lets in a warm glow.

The original magnificent proportions of the rooms in Philippe Model's seventeenth-century Parisian mansion, built by Jules Hardouin-Mansart circa 1646, are embellished by a paint treatment in a style reminiscent of an iconic private office Jean-Michel Frank designed in the 1930s. Frank stuck to light and dark wood to create his surreal design, while Model uses a fan of 128 colors. The light furniture can be rearranged frequently, keeping any room from being designated for a single, fixed function.

Like Frank, Model covered the skirting, paneling, and crown molding—the stripes effectively lengthen the walls and visually pull them in to meet the décor. In the grand salon, far left, Erwan Bouroullec's bench and Model's table and stool sidle up to a nineteenth-century mirror. Regitze Bondesen and Bob Hollywood designed the white bench that sits in the same room, left. Model also painted the dapper fireplace surround in the antechamber, above, in curve-hugging pinstripes.

In a two-story Biscayne Bay penthouse overlooking the Atlantic, interior designer Judi Male pairs classic mid-twentieth-century furniture with art by Frank Stella, Robert Motherwell, Helen Frankenthaler, and Sol LeWitt. In the living room, left, a kidney-shaped shag rug echoes the biomorphic shape of Vladimir Kagan's Serpentine sofa. An off-centered Morris Louis painting from the artist's 1960s Unfurled series demonstrates his technique of applying thinned paint to an unframed, inclined canvas to create feathery vertical tracks that loom up and out or fall down and in.

In antique dealer Mark McDonald's upstate New York house a painting by John McLaughlin, once described as a "cagey, elliptical Zen master," has pride of place. "His best paintings, the oils on masonite from 1952 to 1954, effortlessly express the clarity of West Coast light and the calmness of Eastern philosophy," says McDonald. "In contrast to their minimalist imagery, their few perfect colors strike a harmonic tone and, up close, their surfaces have rich textural dimension."

The open interiors of the Pennsylvania weekend house designer Todd Oldham shares with partner Tony Longoria radiate with wide vertical stripes in Creamsicle orange, pea green, putty, and sky blues that visually amplify space. The house's decorative motifs render a vibe that's part freewheeling roller-coaster ride, part cowboy bordello. In the kitchen, center, Oldham glazed a wall with twenty coats of paint before meticulously gluing on Japanese paper cut-outs to form a decorative pattern. Symmetrical to a T, he never dresses a wall in an odd number of stripes.

In 2008 Susan Silton dramatically transformed the exterior of the Pasadena Museum of California Art. Her intervention, *Inside Out*, revolved around the social and cultural significance of stripes and led her to encase the entire building in a multicolored industrial tarpaulin inspired by the striped fumigation tents that routinely crop up over Los Angeles homes. The vibrancy and verticality of the temporary slipcover made the building seem like a weightless, levitating object. Inside the museum, Silton gathered a plethora of housewares, clothing, and art that served as a commentary on the stripe as a ubiquitous, seductive consumable into a market setting—and like any self-respecting bazaar, all the items were for sale.

San Francisco designer Jay Jeffers planned to swathe the walls of this Sonoma pool pavilion, above, in bolts of striped linen, but the budget held him back. Instead he asked decorative painter Philippe Grandvoinet to step in and render the fabric in paint. Grandvoinet incorporated the ceiling's 15-foot pitch into his design, and Jeffers topped it off with a glass Brunelli chandelier. Thanks to the cool rigor of the design a clutch of plaid, chevron, and crosshatched pillows merge into an upholstered Lulu DK sofa without looking overdressed.

In a 5,000-square-foot prewar Park Avenue apartment owned by writer Amy Fine Collins, right, designer Robert Couturier covered the dining room's focal wall in painted stripes, giving dimension to a salon-style arrangement of framed photographs and prints. The designer also chose a striped pattern for its ability to heighten the ceiling, add abstract texture, and accentuate the fluting in Serge Roche's iconic plaster torchère.

Architects Stamberg Aferiat kept the dining room walls of a Park Avenue interior, left, white in anticipation of a 1994 Sol LeWitt mural, *Wall Drawing 743 Vertical Lines, Not Straight, Not Touching, Covering The Wall Evenly*. To double its impact, the architects installed a set of sympathetically colored Verner Panton chairs and a 10-foot-long table; its glass top reflects a pattern reminiscent of cascading confetti.

The brain processes color and form separately, then pieces the information together. The vertical lines in many of Bridget Riley's paintings, including *Rose Rose 9*, 2010, right, "adapt out" or quickly desensitize a viewer's visual system. Then, suddenly, the pattern appears to begin jumping around, causing many to compare Riley's work to discordant music. Tipping the head to one side rectifies visual discomfort by tapping into the as-yet-unaffected section of the brain that processes horizontal lines, making the colors and forms again appear stable and clear. A horizontal painting from the Rose Rose series was also chosen for a London 2012 Olympics poster—the stripes evoke running tracks and swimming lanes.

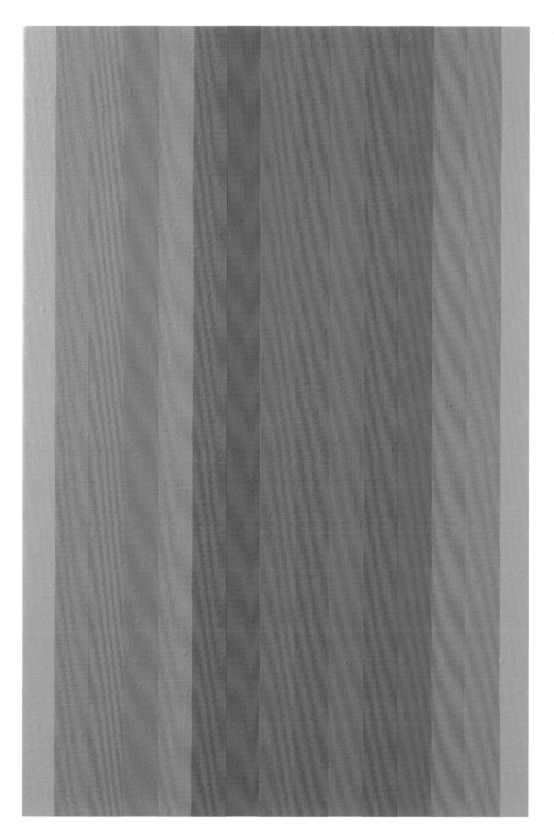

Tailored stripes have the same effect on rooms as bodies. In a renovation of a weekend house on the eastern shore of Long Island, designer Ellen Hamilton installed a long dining table from Holly Hunt, left, and surrounded it with Phoenix Furniture dining chairs. Like a versatile dress, the Perennials striped fabric lends itself to both formal and casual dinners while it grounds the dining area in a space that's essentially open-plan.

Interface carpet's Smithfield Stripe, top, mimics the pattern of a man's suit with its closely placed stripes and low-contrast colors that read as solid from a distance. The company's Blast from the Past carpeting, left, brings to mind a large-scale utilitarian tweed composed of thin stripes in varying widths. It infuses this office floor with dimension, thereby accentuating ceiling height.

Carolyne Roehm themes each guest
room at Weatherstone, her Colonial-
era stone house in Connecticut. In the
Green Room, far left, an upright antique
Swedish clock stands guard before a
sea of military-looking green stripes
that originate just above the baseboards
and envelop the beveled ceiling.

In an Alabama summerhouse located
on a lakeside ninety minutes away
from Birmingham, architect Bill Ingram
skirted the top frame of a pencil-post
bed with a green-and-oatmeal striped
baldachin to evoke a sleeping porch,
left. Outside the room's threshold, a
broadly striped carpet turns a transi-
tional hall into a viewing gallery where
a pair of faux-bamboo Regency chairs
flanks a wall of framed local maps.

Los Angeles architect Aleks Istanbullu
integrated a guesthouse, above, into a
tight, densely landscaped site at the top
of a steep hill in Lago Vista by painting
its fiber-cement panels the same color
as the surrounding canyon grasses. The
855-square-foot structure complies
with the city's strict height and setback
codes, but its vertical patterning defies
any constrictions and lets the building
soar visually.

Over the course of ten weeks mosaic artist Paul J. Marks hand-set 150,000 French porcelain cubes into a striped floor design to optically aggrandize a private party room, above left, in the Hotel Tresanton in St. Mawes, a small Cornish seaside town. A text from *Alice in Wonderland* is incorporated into the perimeter in a palette of several greens and blues.

Design firm Diamond Baratta upholstered a tufted 1950s Giò Ponti chair, left, in two shades of an aqua Ottoman cloth to exaggerate the uniqueness of its sculpted back. The geometric rug shares the same coloration and alludes to landscape maps from the portfolio of Brazilian landscape architect Roberto Burle Marx.

When hat and fantasy shoe designer Philippe Model acquired his seventeenth-century mansion in Paris, he opened up all the rooms to restore them to their former glory. The lofty dining room ceiling, right, now features radiating stripes that mimic a Napoleonic campaign tent—save for the twenty-three telescoping candle holders that cascade down from its ornate central medallion.

Horizontal lines suggest a landscape: it's why perceptual painters avoid them, why architects value them, and why interior designers appreciate the sense of repose they bring to a bedroom, the sense of calm they bring to a waiting room.

Horizontally slatted window blinds lend a room a particularly pleasing sense of symmetry and balance. Ancient Egyptians realized this, and modulated the sun's intensity with angled strips of wood and raised panel shutters that are likely the forerunners of modern Venetian blinds, which reached their highest level of popularity in eighteenth-century Europe. Vertical blinds are easier to clean and technically block light more effectively, but they have less market appeal than their horizontal counterparts because the latter align themselves with a room's windowsills, mantels, curtain railings, and crown moldings and they mingle well with the horizontal lines of a building's facade when viewed from outside.

During the demise of his financial empire, notorious swindler Bernard Madoff regularly reassured employees and investors that he was "steady and true." As if to prove the point, he was often seen on his hands and knees obsessively aligning all the Venetian blind louvers in his office; perhaps Albert Camus was correct, then, when he referred to life as "a horizontal fall."

Frank Lloyd Wright harnessed the power of horizontal lines by bestowing buildings with level roofs, cantilevered planes, and structurally striped stonework, which integrates the structures into the landscape and visually anchors them to their sites. More than a mere building technique, Wright's parallel layering also has a spiritual resonance. "I see this extended horizontal line," he said, "as the true earth-line of human life, indicative of freedom." In much the same way, the yogic expression "God forever rests on the horizon line between all opposites" is a prelude to a third-eye meditation on the meeting point between ocean and sky that promises to expand inner vision.

On a more commercial note, and in a case of prime lateral thinking, Paul Rand based a 1972 modification of the IBM logo he had designed sixteen years earlier on a series of horizontal anti-forgery lines that once defined the signature space on official documents. He incorporated a similar stack of parallel stripes into the new logo, knowing the security and dependability they projected would subliminally become attributes of the company. At the very least, he knew the stripes would suggest speed and dynamism. The "eightstriper," as the now-iconic symbol is called, is said to have reminded one IBM executive of a Georgian chain gang, but decades after its inception, it remains one of the most recognizable—and therefore successful—corporate logos in the world.

Stacked parallel lines also appear frequently in the built world, in the form of entry steps to buildings. These practical features are an architect's way of adding welcoming tiers and layers to a building's imposing vertical facade. That same expansive feeling is reversed, however, in confined spaces, where an excess of horizontal stripes can become oppressive, weighty, and as devoid of life as a conference of flatlines.

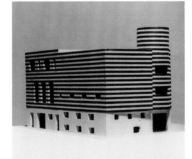

Stripes are a time-honored photographic device for modestly showcasing a woman's curves, far left. Architect Adolf Loos was borderline obsessed with chanteuse/philanthropist Josephine Baker and—unsolicited—he designed a striped house for her in 1927, left. The unbuilt project includes a glass-walled swimming pool surrounded by viewing galleries where Baker could presumably frolic in the nude. The striped Origo pattern, designed by Alfredo Häberli in 1999, below, adorns a wide array of Iittala's bowls, and is one of the Finnish company's most popular patterns.

Despite its name, the proportions of the Motel Grand, right, are anything but. Photographer John Ellis spotted it on the very urban corner of Pico and La Cienega Boulevards in Los Angeles, but it reminded him of a roadside lodging in the middle of nowhere. "At that moment in that particular light, the patchwork of horizontal lines from sky to fascia to sidewalk," he says, "really did come across as grand."

Given free rein inside the Victoria and Albert Museum during the 2011 London Design festival, the Bouroullec brothers created a casual, unintimidating way to view art with their temporary *Textile Field* installation, left. Using foam covered with Kvadrat textiles, they designed a 100-foot-long, gently sloped platform that encouraged viewers to linger, lounge, and recline while they contemplated a gallery of Raphael cartoons.

In *Deconstructing Walls*, right, the Bouroullecs investigate nomadic reconfigurations of space via easily stacked building bricks carved out of cellular foam. Upholstered in multiple shades of Kvadrat fabric, the components piece together like a jigsaw to form bands of color and a seemingly infinite bank of random stripes.

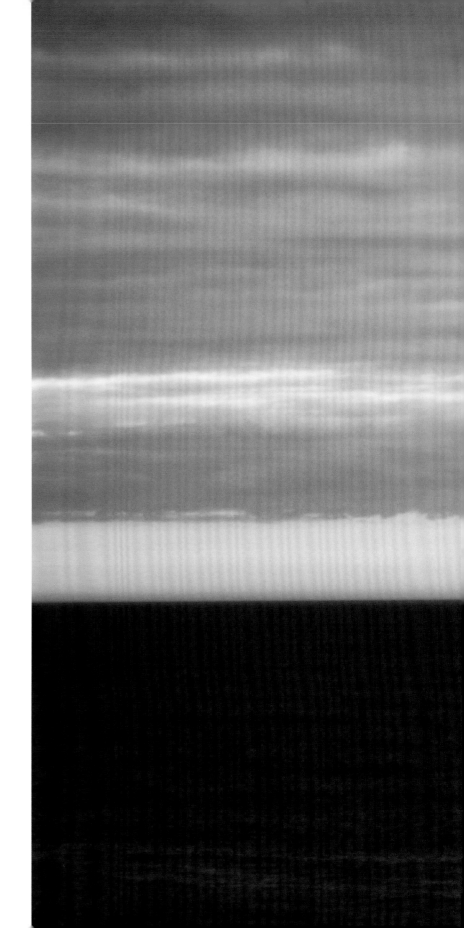

Photographer John M. Hall takes pictures of the ever-changing horizon as seen from the front yard of his house on Long Island, New York. This shot depicts the aftermath of a late-summer storm. Hall's vantage point on a bluff 75 feet above sea level has provided him with enough horizon images to fill a book, *Montauk*. As photographer and acclaimed travel writer Ella Maillart once put it, "The wideness of the horizon has to be inside us, cannot be anywhere but inside us, otherwise what we speak about is geographic distances."

Stripes pop up consistently throughout a house designed by Carolyne Roehm nestled into the western side of Aspen Mountain in Colorado. In the dining room, left, they embolden a linen tablecloth and upholster the seats of neoclassical chairs to supply the room's predominant pattern, conjuring up a fantasy of country life in Gustavian Sweden.

Parisian designer Alberto Pinto encloses a guest bedroom in a Moroccan villa, right, with thick, painted bands of Saharan indigo that complement decoratively plastered vertical beams and fretwork furniture, bringing to mind nomadic desert tents.

A black-tinted cement band snakes its way along the 30-foot-length of a living room in a SoHo penthouse designed by Benjamin Noriega-Ortiz, above, making the space appear twice as long. Its sensual, undulating contour correlates to the mass of plumbing and gas pipes it conceals and also enhances the flames' mesmerizing quality.

The spiral staircase in the inaugural Henry Cotton boutique in Milan, right, draws customers through three floors of merchandise to a central atrium and an elevator shaped like a hot air balloon. London designer Anouska Hempel based her scheme on the clothing brand's association with sports and travel, and unified both pastimes with a striped motif. Stripes are painted on walls and integrated into screens, but they also appear in symmetrical arrangements of vintage wooden oars that once sailed on the Titanic.

Anouska Hempel often lets the architectural symmetry of an unadorned four-poster bed dictate a room's design. Wide horizontal bands intersect the bed's supports, right, and all other elements—linens, headboard, artwork, furniture—fall in line, down to a vase of black-eyed chincherinchees.

In the entrance to a Hamptons house originally conceived by architect Shigeru Ban and reconceptualized by New Yorker Shamir Shah, left, light from an 18-foot-long skylight casts shadows on the gypsum wall, limestone floor, and live-edge walnut bench. At certain times of day it underscores the striped patterning on the silk rug Shah designed. "I didn't plan that," he says. "It was a serendipitous—albeit welcome—surprise."

Despite its strong connection to nature and breathtaking views of Peconic Bay, Muriel Brandolini's 1970s Long Island house emphasizes the angular and boxy. The designer installed floor-to-ceiling horizontal bands on the walls of all the main rooms. In the sitting area, right, the pattern visually converts a landing and a stairwell into one cohesive space: it dictates the placement of library shelves, echoes an orderly arrangement of magazine stacks, and introduces a sense of procession to the hall.

A critic once referred to Liam Gillick's art as familiar, casual, playful, considered, political, and obtuse—in one sentence. The artist merges the disciplines of writing, graphic design, music, filmmaking, and sculpture to produce controversial work he himself has described as "aprofound and quite LITE, as in low-calorie." His clear, modular forms feature stripes as a recurring motif. *STACKED REVISION STRUCTURE*, 2005, far left, is a permanent installation on the grassy grounds of the Albright-Knox Art Gallery in Buffalo, New York, that stands in sharp contrast to the building's neoclassical facade. Powder-coated stacks of aluminum slats create a 12-foot-square cube that confronts visitors as they descend the museum's broad steps.

In *DISCUSSION ISLAND RESIGNATION PLATFORM*, an exhibition from 1997, left, Gillick attached anodized aluminum and Plexiglas pallets to a gallery ceiling to persuade viewers to look up; the treatment caters to his "fondness for diversions and distractions, tangents and evasions."

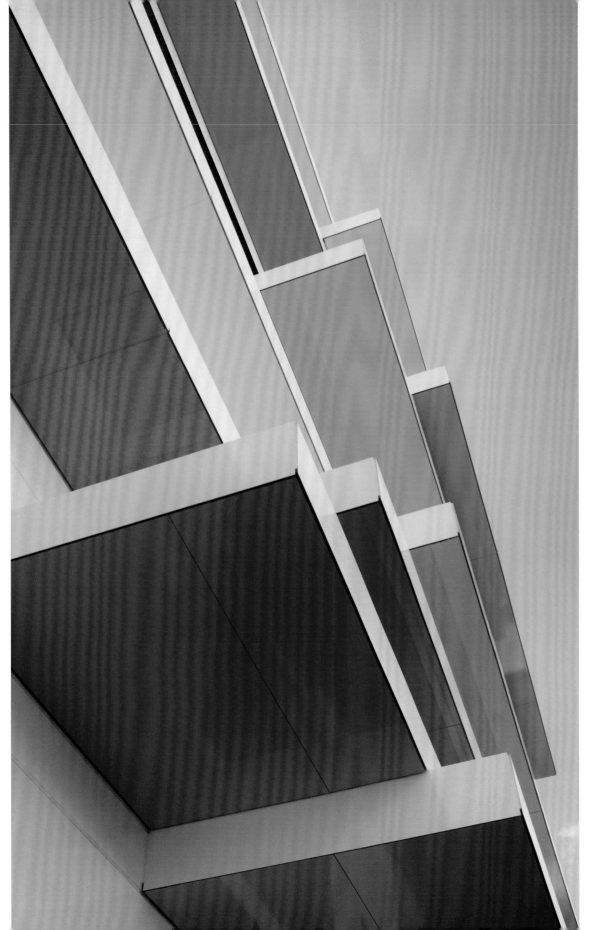

Sliding shoji screens inspired the facade Emmanuelle Moureaux designed for the Shimura branch of the Sugamo Shinkin bank in Japan. The building sits on a chaotic street where the loud noise of traffic reverberates off tall nearby buildings; Moureaux kept her scheme low-rise in contrast and devised an offset, layered facade with gradients of blue on its uppermost layers, to blend into the sky. The exterior palette of twelve colors—inspired by the notion of *shikiri*, or dividing space with color—recurs inside on the upholstery of a casual arrangement of chairs. Depending on the weather at night, the building either glows softly or lights up brightly.

Mary McDonald's Hollywood Regency guesthouse doubles as her design lab. In a basement floor media room, far left, a black-and-pink floral pillow dictates the color palette of the focal wall just behind. The resulting hand-painted stripes draw the eye outside through open doors onto a patio, then beyond to a compact dining pavilion.

Nisi Berryman composes livable vignettes at Niba, her Miami store, to provide customers with furnishing options they can readily apply in their own interiors. Handblown glass with a repoussé copper sculpture and *Forest*, a William Betts painting, form one such tableau, left. Using techniques based on the elasticity of digital imagery, Betts assigns colors to scanned visuals of landscapes and feeds them into a printer that's fuelled with acrylic paint rather than ink.

Near Pretoria, South Africa, Neill and
Cornel Strydom chose striped wallpaper
for the living room fireplace surround
and entry hall wall of their weekend
farmhouse. The same wall treatment
provides visual glue for an animated mix
of Gustavian, midcentury modern, rus-
tic, and Renaissance-inspired furnishings and art deeper in the interior.

The formality Topher Delaney builds into
her landscaping paradoxically enhances
the lush wildness of her plantings. In a
vast garden set into the northern hills of
Hillsborough, California, stripes of color
are both deeply embedded and superfi-
cially delightful. Cultivated rows of baby
tears separate cast concrete pavers,
and a meandering striped wall cordons
off the driveway. After receiving a dapper coat of stripes, a pair of common
storage bins—with castors stabilized in
beds of gravel—becomes a structural
anchor in a courtyard, where they prove
to be sculptural and utilitarian at once.

Horizontal and vertical lines are integral to the structure of every building; when emphasized or left exposed, they illustrate a reassuring alliance between strength and beauty. They exaggerate breadth, add grandeur, unite surfaces, and establish a perpendicular perspective that relates to human scale.

The decoratively striped construction of many Christian churches and cathedrals harkens back to an Islamic and Byzantine tradition, where it probably developed as an economical way to incorporate rare stones with common materials. Late Medieval Italian cathedrals exhibit some of the earliest and most memorable striped facades: Orvieto's features bands of light and dark stone while Siena's is constructed from white and greenish-black marble in alternating stripes. High Victorian architecture took inspiration from this tradition, and a trend of similar patterning and banding in brick spread across nineteenth-century Europe and as far as Australia.

In the 1980s and 1990s, postmodern architects including Robert Venturi used appliquéd planes and stripes of white brick to ornament and integrate facades with their neighboring buildings. For an art gallery in Japan wedged onto a triangular site, architect Mario Botta employs alternating horizontal bands of concrete and granite to help the structure exude permanence and durability on a heavily trafficked, transient street. He has also used horizontal stripes to exaggerate the scale of a modest building and to anchor a house onto a steeply sloping site. The pink and yellow terra-cotta cladding on one of British architect James Stirling's most memorable buildings, Number One Poultry, helps to resolve some functional problems, but it is predominantly decorative, prompting Londoners to call it a "monumental piece of Lego."

In an urban environment, a striped front elevation always draws attention to a building as man-made, but cladding in a rural surrounding that echoes a motif of pastoral life can help a building blend into the broader, natural landscape. Corrugated metal roofs on barns may mimic the furrows in a nearby field, for example, and a shingled cedar sheath on a beach house may relate to the form of a rippled sand dune nearby.

As essayist John Ruskin points out, the vertical and horizontal lines of an edifice will always underscore the involvement of a human hand, but interestingly "the stripes of a zebra do not follow the lines of its body or limbs." Nature uses stripes liberally on

200 the tiniest insects and the largest cats, and has as far back as the era of the dinosaurs—one species of flying reptiles had brightly striped plumage. Stripes are the "fingerprints" of the animal kingdom, and they serve as unique identifiers for each and every tabby cat, snake, badger, and bee.

In the world of flora, blooms with stripes along their petals' veins are known to entertain more pollinating bumblebees than monochromatic flowers. The striped pigment attracts the bees, provides them with a highly visible "landing strip," and advertises the path to a stash of nectar.

Stefano Mantovani's room sets from the 1980s, far left—including this imaginary scheme to envelop a bathroom interior with a plethora of stripes—recall the pop art movement from two decades earlier. The fleshy panicles of a two-tone Heliconia contain abundant nectar for hummingbirds From a distance a bee in its furry fatigues, bottom right, is often mistaken for a wasp, whose stripes are defensive full-body combat gear. Artist Yvonne Gregory, the wife of photographer Bertram Park, posed and likely came up with the idea for this tribute to dazzle painting, below left, in 1914.

Many of the Buddhist temples in Bagan, Myanmar, have long, circumnavigating corridors with colonnades of pillars and exposed structural ceiling beams. The pronounced vertical and horizontal lines of the structure and the shadow lines made by the sun, right, have religious meaning, and establish a metaphysical foundation for the spiritual practice of meditation—the long vistas represent the endless wisdom of Buddha. Interior designer Vicente Wolf describes the architecture as a "perfect example of light geometry."

Formal French parterre gardening, with its carefully pruned and coppiced plants, has three structural principles at its core: horizontal planes, vertical planes, and punctuation points. On a Darien, Connecticut, property close to an expanse of water facing Long Island Sound landscaper Rob Wilber maintains acres of manicured shrubs that trap and expose stripy paths of light. Boxwood pruned into cone shapes and pleached into hedges snake around a dwarf lilac tree, and a forcefully vertical tree trunk intersects the strongly cubic shape of another boxwood hedge.

205

In *Quonset Shed With Bench Near
Yuba City*, 1999, far left, David
Stark Wilson shows the unadorned,
straightforward, weathered parallel
lines of utilitarian architecture. To him
these types of structures represent
the arrival of commerce, which in turn
destroys natural wetlands and fields
of wildflowers. "The land formed them
and they formed the land," he says.

For an Old Greenwich, Connecticut,
house workshop/apd covered the
exterior of a mudroom, left, with
a horizontal ipê wood rain screen.
This treatment helps to integrate
it with the rest of the house and
garage, turning a potentially awkward
architectural transition into a simple,
pleasing geometrical form.

The first striped iceberg Norwegian sailor Oyvind Tangen photographed from the deck of a research vessel as it sailed 1,700 miles south of Cape Town, South Africa, was 150 feet long and 30 feet high, but it reminded him of humbug, the pin-striped candy he liked as a child. The colored striations and bands that decorate subsequent ice masses he's documented likely formed after layers in the ice mass trapped windblown dust and soil as they melted and refroze. Blue stripes may be the result of compressed snow or melt water after it filled a berg's crevice and rapidly responded to arctic temperatures. Green lines are created by salty seawater that contains rich algae colonies. Brown, black, or yellow tracks document sediment picked up when ice sheets grind downhill toward the sea.

Dennis Hodges eschews the traditional symmetry that architectural photographers conventionally use; as a result his detailed shots of buildings are reductive, abstracted essays about illusion, light play, ornamentation, and geometry. He vividly conveys the commanding presence of the Bacardi Building in Havana, Cuba, left, by capturing it as a dynamically diagonal testament to stability and security. By zeroing in on the intense ornamentation of its tiered rectangular pagodas, he acknowledges the Wat Pho Temple in Bangkok, Thailand, upper right, as a rich repository of Thai culture. By reducing the facade of the legendary Gran Hotel La Perla in Pamplona, Spain, right, to a mass of scaffolding and window braces, he deflates the pomp of a five-star establishment.

For the most part the universe's architecture doesn't create rigidly straight lines; the layers, rings, veins, and ripples that convey the personality or age of a natural material or phenomenon are most often freeform. In 2011, however—with a four-and-a-half-hour exposure—photographer Kurt Lawson captured the trajectory of stars traversing the skies above the Sierra Nevadas and nearby Alabama Hills, left, in a way that makes them look linear. "This view to the west shows them as perfectly straight lines," he says, "while a view to the north or south would show the stars circling the earth's axis." Lawson's detailed photograph of veining in the rock slopes beneath the Pemaquid Point Lighthouse in Bristol, Maine, from 1994, upper right, also depicts stripes, and demonstrates a relationship between the bedrock's textural intensity and the ocean waves nearby.

In a sprawling garden Topher Delaney designed on a steep hillside in San Rafael, California, an elliptically shaped pool has walls constructed from complementary shades of blue glass tiles that form a bar code–like pattern that spells out "In Deep Immersion."

Designers have always perceived nature as an antidote to technology and a remedy against impersonal standardization. Whenever a man-made structure or object embodies the characteristics of a natural form it becomes structurally logical, uses materials efficiently, and is deemed innovative to boot. Architect Jeanne Gang used standard concrete, metal, and glass to construct the Aqua apartment tower in the center of Chicago, top right, with lyrical results. The design of this vertiginously tall building, at 82 stories, is anything but arbitrary: its paper-thin undulating balconies deflect the path of strong, potentially hazardous winds. To the casual observer the winds seem to have already left their ripple marks or to have inspired the overall shape, but Gang's idea actually came from striated limestone outcroppings, a common topographical feature of the Great Lakes.

The sculptural doors of the Blend armoire Karim Rashid designed for Horm, right, appear to have the mutability of an Issey Miyake pleated fabric but are in fact made of technologically savvy, evenly spaced, bicolor sheets of medium-density fiberboard.

The sinuous ridges that streak diagonally across a photograph Kurt Lawson took of Death Valley's Mesquite Flat Dunes, far right, are top-coated with a feathery layer of always-moving sand.

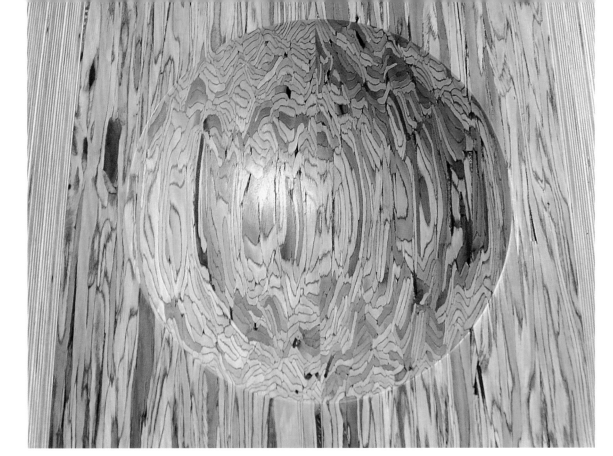

Bristlecone pines have a very slow rate of regeneration and are capable of reaching an age that's greater than any other single living organism known. An exposed trunk, left, appears charred, but according to photographer Kurt Lawson, it is very much alive and its stripy rings indicate that it is thousands of years old.

At their best, designs derived from the outward forms of nature also tap into its essence. By scooping out a section of his Clamp table, top right, designer Harry Allen showcases both the inner and surface materiality of Baltic birch plywood.

Finnish designer and sculptor Tapio Wirkkala always let the metal, glass, ceramics, or plywood he worked with dictate the shape of the artful housewares he created. "All materials," he said, "have their own unwritten law." He designed his iconic Leaf platter, right, in 1951 from laminated birch and held it together with the same gluing technology he'd observed being used in the construction of wooden airplane propellers.

Biomimicry is so compelling because the beautifully repetitive, orderly and uniform design strategies in nature are always based on profound reason. Dennis Hodges's photograph reveals the ribbed chambers of an ammonite's fossilized coiled shell, above, which helped the sea creature dive deep enough to catch its prey.

Judith Turner photographs banana leaves, right, with the same reverence as she does architecture or sculpture. The plant's pin-striped ridges supply structural strength and, an integral part of the plant's well-ordered hydration system, they encourage the absorption of rainwater and moisture.

A cactus's spines, right, are leaves modified for their extreme climate, and the ribs in its stems allow the plant to expand to store water and breathe. Together they keep hungry herbivores at bay and provide the succulent with innovative ventilation.

The billions of bulbs planted every year in parks like Keukenhof and farms on the outskirts of Amsterdam yield spring crops of leggy tulips with voluptuous petals. The fields of orderly rows resemble Technicolor-striped blankets from the air and represent Holland's largest tourist attraction. This cultural tradition stems from the seventeenth century, the country's golden age, when certain rare bulbs could command prices equivalent to an average year's salary.

Since 1979, Judith Turner has been photographing columns. She distorts their scale and sometimes switches the fore- and backgrounds. By training her lens on a detail rather than the overall monolith the familiar becomes temporarily unrecognizable, but the ambiguity soon passes when the fragment is identified as part of a more familiar whole. The resulting imagery has the depth and texture of complex, striped fabric.